D1519038

SAGE CONTEMPORARY
SOCIAL SCIENCE ISSUES
9

EMERGING
THEORETICAL
MODELS
IN SOCIAL AND
POLITICAL
HISTORY

Edited by

Allan G. Bogue

OTHER VOLUMES IN **SAGE ISSUES**

SAGE CONTEMPORARY SOCIAL SCIENCE ISSUES 9

EMERGING THEORETICAL MODELS IN SOCIAL AND POLITICAL HISTORY

Edited by

Allan G. Bogue

SAGE PUBLICATIONS *Beverly Hills / London*

PUBLISHER'S NOTE

The material in this publication originally appeared as a special issue of AMERICAN BEHAVIORAL SCIENTIST (Volume 16, Number 5, May/June 1973). The Publisher would like to acknowledge the assistance of the special issue editor, Allan G. Bogue, and his contributors in making this edition possible.

For information address:

SAGE PUBLICATIONS, INC.
275 South Beverly Drive
Beverly Hills, California 90212

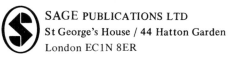

SAGE PUBLICATIONS LTD
St George's House / 44 Hatton Garden
London EC1N 8ER

Printed in the United States of America

International Standard Book Number 0-8039-0321-9

Library of Congress Catalog Card No. 73-87857

FIRST PRINTING (this edition)

CONTENTS

EMERGING THEORETICAL MODELS IN
SOCIAL AND POLITICAL HISTORY

Editor's Introduction

During the late 1950s, historians began to detect a new empirical emphasis in certain areas of their discipline in the United States and began to speak of the new economic history and—somewhat later—of the new political or the new social history. This "new" history of course bore little resemblance to the "new history" of an earlier era of American historiography and the hard-worked adjective's meaning has sometimes been confused in recent years by other or more general uses. Nor has "new" meant quite the same thing in the various subareas of the history discipline. Quantification was usually involved, but economic historians achieved an unexampled merger of economic theory and quantitative and statistical expertise while the theoretical component was much less evident in the work of political historians and still rarer in the writing of the new social historians.

It seems clear that practitioners of the "new" histories all share a commitment to using, refining, and expanding the social science component in the history discipline. Of course, calls for both quantification and an interdisciplinary orientation have echoed down the corridors of the discipline from the late nineteenth century onward, but unprecedented numbers have responded during the last fifteen years. Surveying the trend at the end of the 1960s, the authors (Landes et al., 1971: 73) of the volume on history in *The Behavioral and Social Sciences Survey* (BASSS) entitled their relevant chapter, "Varieties of Interdisciplinary and Social

Scientific History" and suggested that the major characteristics of social scientific history were "aggregation, the marriage of theory and empiricism, and systematic comparison." This characterization is plausible, although it does not prepare the reader for the great variety of quantitative methodologies in use nor the extremely uneven distribution of the specified characteristics in the literature. Although Landes and his coauthors did a good job in describing the characteristics of social scientific history, they were less successful in portraying the relative importance of its various subspecies.

Institutional developments in the United States during the 1960s reflected the growing interest in a social science approach. Beginning in 1960, an annual "cliometrics" seminar held initially at Purdue University (and much later at the University of Wisconsin) served as a focal point of the new economic history. Articles in the *Journal of Economic History* became increasingly econometric in nature, as did those in *Explorations in Entrepreneurial* (later *Economic*) *History*. During the early 1960s, Lee Benson and others obtained permission from the Council of the American Historical Association to organize an ad hoc Committee on Quantitative Data in History and its members assisted the Inter-University Consortium for Political Research (ICPR) in assembling an archive of machine-readable quantitative political data for the use of interested historians and social scientists. Concerned initially with modern American electoral and legislative data, the committee enlarged its purview in 1967 by reorganizing its membership and sponsoring conferences to survey the quantitative historical sources of European and Third World nations (Lorwin and Price, 1972) as well as American colonial sources. The archival interests of the committee members continue. They have also been interested in encouraging the spread of knowledge about the use of quantitative data and interdisciplinary theory and techniques in history and have organized a successful summer institute on electoral and legislative behavior that was sponsored jointly with ICPR in 1965. Subsequently, ICPR added a special course in quantitative techniques to its summer session offerings.

Meanwhile the Mathematical Social Science Board created a History Advisory Committee under the chairmanship of Robert W. Fogel which began an ambitious program of conferences on research in subject matter areas where the application of social science theory and empirical methods promised high yields. From these conferences, an impressive series of books is emerging (McCloskey, 1971; Aydelotte et al., 1972). The committee also sponsored a summer institute for history graduate students in the methods and models of the social sciences in 1967 and is also interested in developing instructional materials for classroom use.

The materials published in the two established American journals in economic history have reflected the new emphasis in that field. The social science thrust in political and social history is best illustrated by the advent of two new periodicals: *The History Methods Newsletter* (Pittsburgh) and the *Journal of Interdisciplinary History* (MIT). But the new *Journal of Social History* has contributed to the trend, and the editors of many other journals have also been responsive.

Articles by the dozens and a substantial and growing list of books attest to the spread of social science history. Some established historians have hailed the new insights that they gained from the work of the social science historians while others have expressed serious reservations or protested that the new work was not history. Still others staunchly ignored the new developments or denied that they changed anything, an attitude reminiscent in some cases of the gentleman who denied that the ministrations of a Chinese warlord's executioner had affected him in any way until he was asked to nod his head. Some of the recrimination seems to stem from a holistic view of history that holds, implicitly or explicitly, that historians all do essentially the same things and share the same objectives in their work. Actually, there are many varieties of history, and there is little reason to believe that barbarians speaking in equations will overrun the empire. Symbiosis seems a more appropriate metaphor. And if historians fail to grasp the opportunities inherent in the application of empirical methods and theory in historical context, it seems clear that social scientists will do so. A majority of the economic historians reside professionally in economics departments, and political scientists and sociologists are increasingly interested in longitudinal analysis.

Although the members of the BASSS history committee listed a "marriage of social science theory and empiricism" as one of the major hallmarks of social science history, the contracting principals can hardly be said to be equal in status or power in any but economic history. Certainly in political and social history, the child bride, the bound foot, or even the shotgun often seems the better analogy. On the one hand, there has been much simple number-smashing and, on the other, a good deal of social science theory has been borrowed and used in a highly speculative and unrigorous way. But it has also become clear to many who first became interested in quantification merely as a better means of answering a conventional historical question like "Who were the Radicals during the American Civil War?" that the combination of theory and quantitative techniques opens vast new perspectives and that spelling out relationships in terms of theory or more restricted models reveals flaws in reasoning and lacunae in the evidence that otherwise might be ignored. It has become clear also that much of the research done in the new political and the new social history can benefit immensely if we subject the implicit or explicit theory and models in use to rigorous scrutiny and put some thought to productive alternatives.

This issue is therefore devoted primarily to consideration of the use or possible use of theory and models, implicit or explicit, by practitioners of the new political and social history in the United States. My preference is to consider generalized explanations of human behavior or institutional interaction as theories and more restricted applications of theory, particularly when operationalized, as models. But the terms theory and model have, of course, been defined in many different ways, and the authors of one relevant recent work treat them as virtually synonymous (Davis and North, 1971). Other scholars sometimes use the term model to describe a research design or a relationship between variables without reference to theory. I have not tried to hold the authors in this issue to the same definitions, and their practices to some degree illuminate the state of the arts among social science historians. The lead article—that by Professor McClelland—has been designed to serve as a reference point for what follows. He describes some of the problems involved in the use of theory and models in economic history, the most advanced branch of the discipline in these respects. Professors Wright, Zemsky, and Dykstra review the work done in areas which have attracted heavy traffic in the new political or social history in the United States—electoral behavior, legislative behavior, and community processes. The two remaining contributions look particularly to the future in the discussion of theory which the authors believe historians can use to good advantage in years ahead. J. Rogers Hollingsworth provides an orientation for a theory of the relationships between industrialization and politics, and Lee Benson presents a set of basic propositions in explanation of social conflict in American history.

Although the articles presented here are of necessity restricted in their scope, the editor and authors are hopeful that they will be found to be both dispassionate and critical and perhaps even prophetic of things to come. They touch upon the concerns of a considerable and growing number of historians who are increasingly interested in delineating and occupying some common ground at least with social scientists, and they focus as well upon problems that some social scientists believe can only be illuminated by reinforcing the longitudinal dimension of social science research. Some scholars believe that such convergence may soon produce institutional manifestations in the form of an association of inter-disciplinary or social scientific history. Time will tell.

—Allan G. Bogue
University of Wisconsin

REFERENCES

AYDELOTTE, W. Q. et al (1972) The Dimensions of Quantitative Research in History. Princeton: Princeton Univ. Press.
DAVIS, L. E. and D. C. NORTH (1971) Institutional Change and American Economic Growth. Cambridge, Eng.: Cambridge Univ. Press.
LANDES, D. S. et al. (1971) History as Social Science. Englewood Cliffs, N.J.: Prentice-Hall.
LORWIN, V. R. and J. M. PRICE (1972) The Dimensions of the Past: Materials, Problems, and Opportunities for Quantitative Work in History. Princeton: Princeton Univ. Press.
McCLOSKEY, D. N. (1971) Essays on a Mature Economy: Britain after 1840. Princeton: Princeton Univ. Press.

Model-Building in the
New Economic History

PETER D. McCLELLAND
Cornell University

Of all varieties of history the economic
is the most fundamental. Not the most important:
foundations exist to carry better things.
How a man lives with his family, his tribe
or his fellow-citizens; the songs he sings;
what he feels and thinks when he looks at the
sunset; the prayers he raises—all these are
more important than the nature of his tools,
his trick of swapping things with his neighbours,
the way he holds and tills his fields, his inventions
and their consequences, his money—when he has
learnt to use it—his savings and what he does
with them [Clapham, 1957: introduction].

As the quotation from Sir John Clapham suggests, economic history is concerned with production and distribution through time.[1] These are the explananda—the phenomena to be explained. What techniques should be used in attempting that explanation has been a subject of lively debate within the profession for over a decade. A revolution is not so much under way as a fait accompli, comprised mainly of new devices for attacking old problems. The first question to be examined is what is new in the "new economic history." The second concerns the extent to which novelty has been synonymous with progress.

THE NEW ECONOMIC
HISTORY: PROBLEMS OF DEFINITION

To begin: What is new? In 1960, a former editor of *Explorations in Entrepreneurial History* concluded that economic history had gained an enviable respect and prestige among the members of the historical profession, primarily because of research accomplishments of the previous decade directed toward the topic aptly summarized by the title of that journal. With a note of regret, he added that the linkage with economic theory remained tenuous, many economic historians knowing "little economic theory and [finding] no use for what they do know" (Aitken, 1960: 87). How curious that latter statement appears today. *Explorations in Entrepreneurial History* (second series) is now entitled *Explorations in Economic History*. Schumpeterian entrepreneurs have all but vanished from its pages before an onslaught of equations, correlation coefficients and partial derivatives. Similar recondite symbols dominate every other major periodical in the field. The founding fathers of this new wave are, first and foremost, professional economists. To their banners have rallied younger colleagues armed with matrix algebra, simulation techniques, and whatever other slings and arrows can be borrowed from the pure theoretician. The resulting cerebral blitzkrieg has been, for most historians, largely unintelligible and not a little disconcerting. Even older members of this new guard, as they survey their protégés at academic conferences must occasionally be tempted to echo Wellington's sentiments on the eve of Waterloo: "I don't know what effect these troops will have on the enemy, but they frighten me" (Nef, 1944: 1).

The timing of the initial transformation remains obscure. It has been variously dated from seminal articles appearing in 1955, 1957, or 1958 (Hughes, 1965; Davis, 1968). The accompanying debate is reminiscent of those attempts to date the inauguration of the clipper ship era from the launching of a single vessel. A major evolution in design takes time, although in retrospect the intellectual transformation was accomplished with startling rapidity. By the middle of the 1960s, a mere handful of architects had restructured the craft of economic history and provocatively reclassified their blueprints "cliometrics." This neologism presumably was meant to signify the marriage of Clio, the muse of history, with that modern deity, Measurement. Historians of more conventional bent were quick to suggest a relationship less flattering—and less voluntary—that a marriage. The union, however, was here to stay.

In its wake have come the predictable spate of articles endeavoring to define, clarify, or denigrate its novel aspects (Davis, 1968; Fogel, 1966; Fishlow and Fogel, 1971; Gerschenkron, 1967; North, 1965; Wright, 1971a), multiple changes being rung on three controlling themes:

(1) the use of economic theory in general and model-building in particular,

(2) the reliance upon quantification to buttress those models with historical data, and

(3) the use of statistical theory, econometrics, and the computer to combine models with data in a single consistent explanation.

All three would seem to be integral parts of the cliometrician's methodology, with the *pervasive* use of the first and third very much a development of recent years.

No article can hope to survey thoroughly a literature which is not only vast, but expanding at the speed of the printing press. It follows that generalizations about dominant trends, past and future, will always do violence to some of the major contributions in the field. The objective of this article is therefore quite modest: to outline some of the new analytical devices now being employed by specialists in a social science which, whether dismal or not, does show signs of becoming esoteric.

The cliometric tools to be examined include three models and one arithmetic device. The models are (1) input-output analysis (2) supply and demand analysis, and (3) growth models. The arithmetic device merely postulates certain constancies in order to solve for missing data.

ARITHMETIC DEVICES

To begin with the simplest of these, the arithmetic device, as its name implies, involves no economics whatsoever. The arithmetic procedures may consist of straight-line interpolation, the extrapolation of ratios from one period to another, or econometric curve-fitting. In all cases, the objective is to use the relationship between two or more variables when all of them can be observed to estimate missing data when only some of them can be observed. The legitimacy of any given procedure can only be judged on an ad hoc basis. The postulate of no major changes over a ten-year period in the ratio of raw material purchases to final sales for ante bellum American industry would seem eminently reasonable, especially when applied to industries that have experienced little technological progress in the interim (Gallman, 1960). The extrapolation of interregional trade patterns of the 1880s to America of the 1850s is considerably less credible (Fogel, 1964b). The key question is always whether other historical evidence indicates that too many relevant variables have changed too much between the period of missing data and the period of observed data. The larger the change, the greater is the probable distortion from assuming whatever constancy is implied in the arithmetic procedure.

Evaluating the worth of cliometric models also requires some attempt to determine the legitimacy of assumptions imbedded in each model. The procedure once again is to scrutinize the correspondence between assumptions and historical reality—or, more correctly, between assumptions and other evidence concerning the historical process under study. Because all assumptions necessarily involve abstraction, no exact correspondence is likely to be observed. Judgment is therefore inevitably introduced in much the same way it is introduced into the assessment of arithmetic devices. The issue is how much divergence is too much, and that will depend critically upon the extent to which observed divergences imperil the model's ability to explain what it purports to explain.

INPUT-OUTPUT MODELS

The key assumptions of input-output analysis are really two in number:

(a) all goods are produced under constant returns to scale; i.e., if all inputs are doubled, output will double; and

(b) each good can be produced by only one combination of inputs, or one fixed recipe relating inputs and outputs.

For analyzing the probable impact of small changes in demand upon a complex industrial structure over a short time period, the tool is without a serious competitor. The larger the proposed change and the longer the time period, the more uneasy one becomes about the rigidity implied by the assumptions. A counterfactual postulating a radical shift in demand raises immediately the question of whether available factor supplies could have met that demand. (Input-output analysis per se indicates nothing whatsoever about the probable answer.) If the hypothesis cum input-output analysis concerns both a radical shift and a prolonged time period, further doubts enter concerning the assumed inflexibility in production coefficients. Abundant factors of production can and do replace scarce factors over time, and technological progress frequently reduces the use of both. "The crucial question is not whether coefficients of production are, in a descriptive sense, rigorously fixed—quite obviously they are not—but whether treating them as if they were yields good predictions" (Friedman, 1955: 171)—and for our purposes, good historical explanations.

Even if all its assumptions are deemed acceptable for the

problem under study, input-output analysis is singularly unhelpful in (a) explaining why demand changed (demand changes are taken as exogenously given), (b) analyzing the determinants of basic factors of production (these too are determined by forces outside the model), and (c) analyzing the causes and effects of technical change (the fixed coefficients of production imply an absence of technical change). Add to these reservations the fact that constructing an input-output table is a horrendous statistical undertaking, and one is not surprised to find that the tool is seldom used by practitioners of the new economic history. The discussion must therefore turn—as the cliometrician frequently turns—to models that incorporate both supply and demand factors in a single consistent explanation of a range of historical phenomena.

SUPPLY AND DEMAND MODELS: DEMAND

The second type of model usually has as its objective the resolution of a puzzle which might be characterized as follows: Historians assert that factors C_1, C_2, and C_3 (for example, population growth, falling prices, and income expansion) were instrumental in causing the change in a given variable E from E_1 to E_2 (such as the increase in British textile production from 100 million yards a year to one billion yards). Can one partition the effects of these three factors and designate how much of the change from E_1 to E_2 is attributable to each one?

The basic procedure followed is summarized in any introductory textbook in economics that presents a picture of shifting supply and demand curves in two dimensions. The independent variable is price; the dependent variable is the quantity demanded. The contribution of falling price (e.g., the price decline occasioned by technological progress) to the observed increase in the quantity sold is indicated by the intersection of the new supply curve (i.e., the one incorporating the new technology) with the old demand curve (i.e., the one excluding those nonprice factors that shifted the demand curve—in our example, the factors population growth and rising incomes). The net result indicates how much demand would have increased if prices had fallen and population and income had remained constant. The partitioning of other causal factors involves this same technique applied in several dimensions rather than two. The critical problem in implementing this technique is to determine the shapes of the supply and demand curves for the commodity being analyzed.

Most cliometric models assume that the demand curve is log-linear in shape. That is, if Q, P and Y stand for the quantity demanded, price, and income, respectively, and if one believes that demand is a function of price and income or that

$$Q = f(P, Y)$$

then this causal assertion would be transformed into

$$\log.Q = a + b \log.P + c \log.Y$$

using the general equation for a straight line learned by most high school students in introductory algebra. Geometrically, this is equivalent to assuming that demand curves are linear, but with the axes now reading "logarithm of price" and "logarithm of quantity"; hence, the name "log-linear demand curve." Once the general shape of the curve has been specified, one can solve for the values of the small letters, or parameters, "a," "b," and "c," using statistical theory, available data, and a computer. The goal is to find that log-linear curve which best fits the data in the sense that the observed divergence—or more correctly, the sum of the squared divergences—from actual data to the line fitted to that data is minimized.

The assumption that the demand curves of economic reality are log-linear in shape is common to most cliometric models that include demand factors in their explanatory variables (Fogel and Engerman, 1971; Pope, 1972; Wright, 1971a, 1971b). The assumption itself is seldom justified explicitly, and such infrequent justifications as are offered emphasize "goodness of fit" in the sense that the estimated log-linear equation closely approximates the observations which the equation is designed to explain (Fogel and Engerman, 1971: 153). Occasional reference is also made to the "goodness of fit" achieved by similar equations employed in recent studies of twentieth-century consumption data. The charm of the equation itself, as enunciated by one of the pioneers in its use (Houthakker, 1965: 278), is mainly "goodness of fit, ease of estimation, and immediacy of interpretation."

To historians, the equation may seem to be nothing more than a figment of the cliometrician's imagination, bearing no apparent relationship to the real world. The reply is to ask what evidence would indicate a relationship with the real world. The historian's own methodology consists of nothing more than advancing hypotheses and then demonstrating that surviving evidence is consistent with those hypotheses. Surely the same procedure is being followed here. The equation *is* the hypothesis, and goodness of fit is equivalent to demonstrating the consistency of surviving *numerical* evidence with that hypothesis. The historian must of course decide whether the general causal assertions of the equation are believable. Once he concedes the relevance of the causal factors in the equation; or, put another way, once he agrees that demand is influenced by those variables listed on the right-hand side of the equation; then the determination of how those variables influenced demand can only be settled by postulating a specific form for the equation and observing how well that form fits the data. The real dilemma occurs when two or more different equations fit the data about equally well. This is analogous to that conventional dilemma of historical analysis: how to choose between two competing hypotheses when surviving historical evidence is consistent with both of them.

Current research by econometricians (as distinct from cliometricians) is now focusing on alternative equation forms which fit contemporary consumption data as well as, or better than, the log-linear demand system (Yoshihara, 1969; Parks, 1969). The relevance of these alternative forms for historical analysis has yet to be explored by practitioners of the new economic history. The one serious attempt to test alternative equation systems on nineteenth-century American data led to discouraging results. In 1875, the Massachusetts census collected information on the incomes and expenditures of 397 families in the state. Jeffrey Williamson (1967: 113) tested these data against three different demand equations, each of which implied "quite different things about household behavior." His main conclusion was that "in terms of goodness of fit, it is difficult to discriminate among the three functional forms except that for food, and one of its components, groceries, the log-linear function is definitely inferior" (Williamson, 1967: 115). Despite these latter reservations, Williamson chose the log-linear equation for his later analysis, essentially because of its convenient properties.

To review, the goodness of fit of log-linear demand equations used to date in cliometric models does indicate a consistency of numerical evidence with the hypotheses embedded in the specific equations. The better the fit, the more consistent is the evidence. What remains unknown is whether alternative equations would fit the data even better.

SUPPLY AND DEMAND MODELS: SUPPLY

Two different sets of assumptions dominate the supply side analysis of cliometric models. The more simple of the two—the combination of perfect competition with constant costs—is evoked when the only problem is to specify the general shape of the supply function. The implied shape is a horizontal straight line. If the assignment is to partition the relative importance of causal forces operating on the supply side, the usual assumptions are perfect competition plus a Cobb-Douglas production function.

The general purpose of any production function is to express the relationship between inputs used and output created. The Cobb-Douglas production function assumes that these relationships can be portrayed by a log-linear curve. That is, if output (0) is a function of two inputs, labor (L) and capital (K), plus an index of total factor productivity (A), then this general causal assertion $0 = F(A,L,K)$ can once again be transformed into

$$\log.0 = \log.A + x \log.L + y \log.K.$$

The function usually appears in the literature in its non-logarithmic form, or as,

$$0 = A L^x K^y.$$

The first equation is simply the logarithmic transformation of the second. The meaning of A will perhaps be more apparent if the terms of the second equation are rearranged to give

$$A = \frac{0}{L^x K^y}.$$

The value of A expresses the relationship between factor inputs and output. If the latter doubles while factor inputs remain the same, then the index A would double, indicating a doubling in productivity. The equation itself is called a Cobb-Douglas production function after the two men (Cobb, a mathematician, and Douglas, an economist) who first advanced it as a possible description of economic reality. If it does describe the production conditions either for a given industry or for an entire nation, then the equation can be used to determine how much of the observed increase in output is attributable to increased use of factor inputs, and how much to an unexplained residual labeled "technological change" or "productivity." Available space does not permit both a detailing of how this is achieved and an assessment of the merits of the technique used. What follows is simply a brief survey of problems that arise in assessing the worth of the supply assumptions of cliometric models.

To begin with the first set—perfect competition plus constant costs: The assumption of constant costs, although frequently made, is seldom defended. When it is, reference is usually made to the ready availability of factor supplies—a circumstance that should minimize variation in input prices as the output of the industry rises and falls (Fogel and Engerman, 1971: 156-157; Temin, 1964: 32). In their study of the ante bellum iron industry, Fogel and Engerman (1971: 156) also cite the observed constancy in the average size of firm and the absence of evidence suggesting that larger firms were more likely to survive—both observations consistent with an absence of economies of scale, and therefore an absence of decreasing costs (as opposed to constant costs).

The assumption of perfect competition, also frequently made, is infrequently defended by reference to the number of firms in the industry under study as being "large." Additional support can on occasion be marshalled by reference to prevailing foreign competition in those markets in which the industry is attempting to sell its products. Perfect competition is not one assumption but three: knowledge is perfect, the product is standardized, and no participant in the market is large enough to affect market variables directly. These conditions are seldom, if ever, met. The assumption of perfect competition may nevertheless provide a useful explanation of market behavior (Eckaus, 1972: 72):

> If there are a "reasonable" number of alternative buyers and sellers.
>
> If the effect on the market of the entry or withdrawal of a few of them is not "appreciable."
>
> If buyers are "reasonably" well informed about quality differences.

The problem once again is to decide how much divergence is too much, and that decision will hinge—once again—upon what the model purports to explain.

The assumption of perfect competition is used by Peter Temin (1964: 344-351) in his analysis of the ante bellum iron industry of western Pennsylvania, from which he infers (a) that prices closely approximated real costs of production, and therefore (b) that observed movements in price could be considered indicative of changing supply conditions. The same assumption of an identity between price and costs becomes considerably more suspect when applied to the steel industry of the late nineteenth century or to the American railroad sector of 1890 (Temin, 1964; Fogel, 1964b; McClelland, 1968). How much competition diverged from perfect and how much prices diverged from costs is of course the central question in both cases. The tradition of science—and, presumably, of a social science—is that he who asserts must offer proof of those assertions. When the price-cost relationship of perfect competition is used to analyze an industry featuring the likes of Andrew Carnegie or J. J. Hill, the cliometrician would seem under some obligation to offer evidence demonstrating that the apparent marked divergence of reality from his assumptions does not affect his ultimate conclusions. Without that evidence, the merits of both the model and its conclusions remain obscure. The same caveat applies to the assumption of constant costs. The image of the ante bellum iron industry expanding and contracting its output without seriously affecting the price of factor inputs is not likely to be contested by most historians of the period (Temin, 1964). The image of 79.2 billion ton-miles of railroad freight being rediverted to alternative carriers in 1890 without affecting the per-unit costs of those alternative carriers has considerably less appeal (Fogel, 1964). Here, too, the cliometrician who asserts what is not intuitively obvious has an obligation to marshal evidence demonstrating that any probable divergence of reality from his assumptions is unlikely to significantly affect his final conclusion.

What of the second pair of assumptions common to supply-side analysis? The combination of perfect competition with the assumption of an industrywide or nationwide Cobb-Douglas production function raises a complicated assessment problem. It begins with yet another construct of economic theory—in this case, the elasticity of substitution, which measures how easily factors of production can be substituted for one other. (The equation defining the elasticity of substitution is somewhat complex, and need not be elaborated for purposes of this discussion.)[2] In a world characterized by the constant production coefficients of input-output analysis, output can be created by only one fixed combination or recipe of inputs. Factors cannot be substituted for each other, and the elasticity of substitution is therefore zero. In a world characterized by Cobb-Douglas production functions, the substitution of one factor for another in the production process is extremely easy. The elasticity of substitution in this case happens to be unity, and it is this characteristic which constitutes the most distinctive feature of the Cobb-Douglas production function. Why this is so need not concern us here. One might, however, note in passing that the ease with which factors can be substituted for each other is the reason why the share of each factor in total output should be observed to remain constant over time.

The historian thoroughly confused by the prevalence of jargon and unspecified theoretical inferences need only focus on two points (or accept on faith two assertions). *If* the production process is Cobb-Douglas in structure, *then* one ought to observe that the elasticity of substitution (however it is defined) is not significantly different from unity when available data are subjected to econometric testing. If the production process is Cobb-Douglas in structure *and* markets are highly competitive, then one ought to observe a constancy over time in the share paid to each factor of production. These constitute two independent tests of whether the world is Cobb-Douglas in structure, and one test of whether it is both Cobb-Douglas and highly competitive.

What is the evidence? Cliometric studies of nineteenth-century data on occasion do refer to the constancy of the share paid to each factor of production over time (Fogel and Engerman, 1971: 156; McCloskey, 1970: 450, n.1; Gallman, 1972: 37). Somewhat less frequently cited from modern studies of postwar American manufacturing is evidence that indicates an elasticity of substitution not significantly different from unity when cross-section data are subjected to econometric testing. (Whether or not time series data support the same conclusion is still a subject of debate; Jorgenson, 1972; Bridge, 1971.) If the production process in nineteenth-century American industry resembled that of the modern era, then the modern data—and recent studies of those data—do lend support to the representation of industrywide production conditions by an industrywide Cobb-Douglas production function.

The case for applying the same function to nationwide

analysis is much less convincing. The ignoring of all demand factors—and perforce the ignoring of all Keynesian problems —can be justified only by assuming that, in the long run, supply will create its own demand. For nineteenth-century America, with its flexible price structure and highly competitive environment, that assumption does not appear to be unreasonable. Doubts begin to arise, however, when one notes that nineteenth-century American data do not indicate that the share of total output paid to labor was relatively constant over time, either for the economy as a whole, or for broad subsectors such as agriculture and industry (Budd, 1960: 373). Equally damaging is Lebergott's (1964: 54) contention that such constancy as can be observed may well be a fabrication of the collection procedure. "We find that these data . . . were originally estimated with so many constancies stipulated in the estimation procedure that we can safely conclude nothing from them about the constancy of labor's share." As for the share of other factors of production, "We conclude that the conceptual problem of disentangling capital from labor returns to entrepreneurs makes useless a discussion of labor's share in total national income—as well as in any industry dominated by entrepreneurial activity, such as agriculture, construction, and trade and service."

The challenge does not end here. A key theoretical difficulty is that, if an aggregate production function is to exist at all—if national supplies of a few basic inputs are to be viewed as combining, within the context of a specific production function, to create national output—then one must also assume that production conditions within all firms in the economy are *very* similar with respect to capital used, labor proportions employed, and output created. An exploration of the precise assumptions required would lead the discussion into one of the more thorny paths of economic theory—and unnecessarily so. What is significant for our purposes is that the theoretician who first elaborated those assumptions also noted that, for a diverse economy, they "are far too stringent to be believable" (Fisher, 1971: 305). The same author did concede (1971: 306-307) that *if* the observed share paid to each factor of production remains relatively constant over time, then a nationwide Cobb-Douglas production function—although an artificial construct—will still predict certain macroeconomic variables fairly well. This particular justification for reinstating an aggregate Cobb-Douglas production function into the analysis of long-term growth is unacceptable in the American case for the simplest of reasons: the requisite constancy in factor shares is not supported by available data on those shares.

To review, for industry studies of nineteenth-century America, the assumptions of perfect competition and an industrywide Cobb-Douglas production function can be given at least tenuous support by observations on the multiplicity of firms and the constancy of factor shares in total output, and by twentieth-century studies of American manufacturing which suggest that (at least for the twentieth-century industries examined) the elasticity of substitution of factors of production does not appear to have been significantly different from unity. The same assumptions applied to the nation as a whole will not do. Factor shares do not appear to have been constant over time, and what constancy can be observed is highly suspect given the manner in which the data were initially assembled. Last, but by no means least, the assumptions that one must make to guarantee the existence of *any* aggregate production function are so stringent that these aggregate production functions cannot be regarded even as good approximate descriptions of the manner in which output is generated within a diverse economy. Must one therefore share the pessimism of Bridge (1971: 397) that "any attempt to use production functions for long-run purposes seems bound to fail"?

More believable alternatives appear to be distressingly scarce. Growth models of the Rostow/Lewis-type, relying primarily or exclusively upon the driving force of capital accumulation harnessed to a fixed capital-output ratio, can be dismissed as blatantly inadequate.[3] The historical record contradicts their main empirical assertion: the rate of investment did not rise from five percent or less to ten percent or more of GNP during the formative years of industrialization in the now-developed countries (Kuznets, 1965). Recent studies of twentieth-century data show, at best, a poor correlation between income and investment; at worst, a negative correlation between economic growth and the marginal capital-output ratio (at least in the short run; Leibenstein, 1966). Again, the evidence contradicts the theory—in this case, the postulate of constancy in a nationwide marginal capital-output ratio. This is hardly surprising. To cite only one of a host of problems, what production conditions would allow the expansion in output to be tied so rigorously to variations in capital inputs? One theoretical possibility would be an economy that was heavily endowed with surplus labor, with all production functions featuring fixed technological coefficients of the input-output variety and with all output created by only two inputs: labor and capital. The example merely helps to illustrate the absurdity of assuming a constancy in a nationwide marginal capital-output ratio. As for the overall importance of this particular input to the growth process, the prevailing opinion among development economists is that capital accumulation per se explains very little of the observed long-term growth in per capita income achieved by developed countries, nor is the pattern expected to change in the near future (Morgan, 1969: 397-399).

GROWTH

The driving force usually regarded as the prime contributor to advances in per capita income is technological progress (Hahn and Matthews, 1964; Kennedy and Thirlwall, 1972), and about the origins of this particular variable economists know distressingly little. Whitehead's judgment that "the greatest invention of the nineteenth century was the method of invention" (Jewkes et al., 1958: 58) may seem more rightly applied to the twentieth century, but, however systematized this method has become since the days of Boulton and Watt, the forces determining how it will be administered, to what problems, and with what results, are still largely an unsolved mystery. The difficulty of predicting future inventions, or even of judging the worth of the current stock is suggested by the London *Times* forecast in 1906 that "all attempts at artificial avia- tion . . . are . . . foredoomed to failure," and four years later the announcement by the British Secretary of State for War that "we do not consider that aeroplanes will be of any possible use for war purposes" (Jewkes et al., 1958: 230-231).

The contours of this process are not entirely shrouded in darkness. Current evidence does suggest that profit incentives have some influence on the actions of would-be inventors (Nordhaus, 1969; Nelson, 1959). Jacob Schmookler (1966) has demonstrated that patent activity is positively correlated with changes in the demand for the product which the patented inventions are designed to improve. The inventive process itself, however, is still regarded by most historians as being largely random and capricious—particularly so in those primeval days before the advent of the modern corporation, R & D depart- ments, and the systematic harnessing of science to problems of technology. If correct, this view would effectively preclude the formulation of a rigorous and widely applicable theory of the inventive process. That, in turn, would effectively limit the changes of devising a comprehensive theory of economic growth.

Discussions of how to formulate a theory of economic growth usually begin with a list of the difficulties associated with analyzing developments over a long period of time. Once the theoretician abandons the Marshallian short period, he loses his ability to impound a host of factors under ceteris paribus, and thereby loses the powerful tools of partial equilibrium analysis. The search for alternatives must invariably confront the charge (Myrdal, 1958: 235) that growth theories which focus exclusively upon economic variables are "doomed to be unrealistic, and thus irrelevant." If the above discussion has one central theme, it is that the issue is not this simple. All explanations involve abstraction and all abstractions imply a lack of realism. The baffling, ineluctable question is how much abstraction is too much. Cliometric models incorporating

Cobb-Douglas production functions and log-linear demand curves can yield a set of equations that incorporate a number of the foremost causal mechanisms of economic theory. When applied at the industrywide level, these equations often fit quite well much of the data which they are designed to explain. Growth models based upon aggregate Cobb-Douglas production functions or upon nationwide marginal capital-output ratios may also be found, on occasion, to fit quite well the principal macroeconomic data of a given society. In the latter case, however, neither model would seem to be consistent with much of available evidence, and both require, to be a valid representation of the growth process, a range of assumptions that appear far too stringent to be considered as reasonable first approximations for a diverse economy. Finally, our ignorance about the determinants of that one factor considered central to the growth process—technical change—is nothing short of abysmal. The implied conclusion is both obvious and exasperating. The development economist and economic historian would both welcome new theoretical constructs to facilitate their analysis of long-term change. At least to date, both wait in vain.

Significant progress has been made, but in solving problems of a lesser scope. For the analysis of short-run patterns of undramatic changes, the cliometrician can often apply effectively those assumptions and tools which are the stock in trade of the economic theoretician. Profit-maximizing behavior by operators of small-scale firms producing in highly competitive markets; relatively constant costs for limited variations in output; relative constancy in other production relationships to facilitate the search for missing data—these often appear to constitute reasonable first approximations to economic reality, especially when applied to America of the nineteenth century. Such tools as log-linear demand curves and industrywide Cobb-Douglas production functions may well continue to be effective devices for partitioning the relative importance of those causal forces underlying short-run economic change. The larger goal of partitioning the impact of causal forces underlying long-term economic growth—for many, the most exciting goal of economic history—would seem as yet beyond our grasp.

NOTES

1. The following is condensed from a book in progress entitled *Causal Explanation and Model Building in History, Economics and the New Economic History*. The chapter from which this article is taken is concerned with both explaining and assessing the principal models now being employed in economic history. This article focuses primarily on the latter. The author is particularly grateful to Allan Bogue for his invaluable assistance in effecting that condensation.

2. "The elasticity of substitution . . . tells us how rapidly diminishing returns set in to one factor of production when its price falls relative to another factor price. For two factors of production, labor (N) and capital (C), it is represented symbolically by

$$\sigma = \frac{d(\frac{N}{C})}{(\frac{N}{C})} \div \frac{d(\frac{fC}{fN})}{(\frac{fC}{fN})} \quad ,$$

where fN is the marginal product of labor, and fC is the marginal product of capital. The ratio of the marginal product of capital to the marginal product of labor is the marginal rate of substitution of labor for capital. . . . Hence the elasticity of substitution as defined in the formula relates the proportional change in the relative factor inputs to a proportional change in the marginal rate of substitution between labor and capital. . . . Intuitively, it can be thought of as a measure of the ease of substitution of labor for capital" (Brown, 1966: 18). The nature of the above formula is perhaps more clear if one defines

$$u = \frac{N}{C} \quad \text{and} \quad R = (\frac{\partial x}{\partial C}) \div (\frac{\partial x}{\partial N})$$

Where (x) represents output. The elasticity of substitution is then

$$\sigma = (\frac{du}{u}) \div (\frac{dR}{R}) \quad .$$

3. Where the elasticity of output with respect to *capital* inputs in a Cobb-Douglas model is given by

$$y = (\frac{\Delta O}{O}) \div (\frac{\Delta K}{K}) \quad .$$

The marginal capital-output ratio is defined as

$$\frac{\Delta K}{\Delta O} \quad .$$

It indicates the causal linkage between an absolute increase in capital inputs and the resulting change in total output. One notable difference between the two formulae is that the causal factor, capital, now appears in the numerator rather than the denominator. The substantive difference, however, is that a capital-output ratio postulates a constant relationship between absolute changes, rather than between proportional changes.

REFERENCES

AITKEN, H.G.J. (1960) "On the present state of economic history." Canadian J. of Economics and Pol. Sci. 26 (February): 87-95.

BRIDGE, J. L. (1971) Applied Econometrics. Amsterdam: North Holland.

BROWN, M. (1966) On the Theory and Measurement of Technological Change. Cambridge, Eng.: Cambridge Univ. Press.

BUDD, E. C. (1960) "Factor shares, 1850-1910," in National Bureau of Economic Research (ed.) Trends in the American Economy in the Nineteenth Century, Studies in Income and Wealth 24. Princeton: Princeton Univ. Press.

CLAPHAM, J. H. (1957) A Concise Economic History of Britain. Cambridge, Eng.: Cambridge Univ. Press.

DAVIS, L. E. (1968) "'And it will never be literature': the new economic history: a critique." Explorations in Entrepreneurial History Second Series 6 (Fall): 75-92.

ECKAUS, R. S. (1972) Basic Economics. Boston: Little, Brown.

FISHER, F. M. (1971) "The existence of aggregate production functions." Econometrics 37 (October): 553-577.

FISHLOW, A. and R. W. FOGEL (1971) "Quantitative economic history: an interim evaluation of past trends and present tendencies." J. of Economic History 31 (March): 15-42.

FOGEL, R. W. (1966) "The new economic history: its findings and methods." Econ. History Rev. 19 (December): 642-656.

––– (1964a) "Reappraisals in American economic history: discussion." Amer. Econ. Rev. 54 (May): 377-389.

––– (1964b) Railroads and American Economic Growth. Baltimore: Johns Hopkins.

––– and S. L. ENGERMAN (1971) The Reinterpretation of American Economic History. New York: Harper & Row.

FRIEDMAN, M. (1955) "A review of input-output analysis: comment," pp. 169-174; in National Bureau of Economic Research (ed.) Input-Output Analysis: An Appraisal, Studies in Income and Wealth 18. Princeton: Princeton Univ. Press.

GALLMAN, R. E. (1972) "The pace and pattern of American economic growth," pp. 15-60 in L. E. Davis et al., American Economic Growth. New York: Harper & Row.

––– (1960) "Commodity output, 1839-1899," pp. 13-71 in National Bureau of Economic Research (ed.) Trends in the American Economy in the Nineteenth Century, Studies in Income and Wealth 24. Princeton: Princeton Univ. Press.

GERSCHENKRON, A. (1967) "The discipline and I." J. of Econ. History 27 (December): 443-459.

HAHN, F. H. and R.C.O. MATTHEWS (1964) "The theory of economic growth: a survey." Econ. J. 74 (December): 779-902.

HOUTHAKKER, H. S. (1965) "New evidence on demand elasticities." Econometrica 33 (April): 277-288.

HUGHES, J.R.T. (1965) "A note in defense of Clio." Explorations in Entrepreneurial History 2nd Series 2 (Winter): 154.

JEWKES, J. et al. (1958) The Sources of Invention. London: Macmillan.

JORGENSON, D. W. (1972) "Investment behavior and the production function." Bell J. of Economics and Management Sci. 3 (Spring): 220-251.

KENNEDY, C. and A. P. THIRLWALL (1972) "Technical progress: a survey." Econ. J. 82 (March): 11-72.

KUZNETS, S. (1965) "Notes on the take-off," pp. 22-43 in W. W. Rostow (ed.) The Economics of Take-Off into Sustained Growth. New York: St. Martin's.

LEBERGOTT, S. (1964) "Factor shares in the long term: some theoretical and statistical aspects," pp. 53-86 in National Bureau of Economic Research (ed.) The Behavior of Income Shares, Studies in Income and Wealth 27. Princeton: Princeton Univ. Press.

LEIBENSTEIN, H. (1966) "Incremental capital-output ratios and growth rates in the short run." Rev. of Economics and Statistics 47 (February): 20-27.

McCLELLAND, P. D. (1968) "Railroads, American growth and the new economic history: a critique." J. of Econ. History 28 (March): 102-123.

McCLOSKEY, D. N. (1970) "Did Victorian Britain fail?" Econ. History Rev. 23 (December): 446-459.

MORGAN, T. (1969) "Investment versus economic growth." Econ. Development and Cultural Change 27 (April): 392-414.

MYRDAL, G. (1958) Value in Social Theory: A Selection of Essays on Methodology. London: Routledge & Kegan Paul.

NEF, J. U. (1944) "What is economic history?" J. of Economic History 4 (December): 1-19.

NELSON, R. R. (1959) "The economics of invention: a survey of the literature." J. of Business, University of Chicago 32 (April): 101-127.

NORDHAUS, W. D. (1969) Invention, Growth and Welfare: A Theoretical Treatment of Technological Change. Cambridge, Mass.: MIT Press.

NORTH, D. C. (1965) "The state of economic history." Amer. Econ. Rev. 55 (May): 86-91.

PARKS, R. W. (1969) "Systems of demand equations: an empirical comparison of alternative functional forms." Econometrica 37 (October): 629-650.

POPE, C. (1972) "The impact of the ante-bellum tariff on income distribution." Explorations in Econ. History 9 (Summer): 375-422.

SCHMOOKLER, J. (1966) Invention and Economic Growth. Cambridge, Mass.: Harvard Univ. Press.

TEMIN, P. (1964) Iron and Steel in Nineteenth Century America. Cambridge, Mass.: MIT Press.

WILLIAMSON, J. G. (1967) "Consumer behavior in the nineteenth century: Carroll D. Wright's Massachusetts workers in 1875." Explorations in Entrepreneurial History Second Series 4 (Winter): 98-135.

WRIGHT, G. (1971a) "Econometric studies of history," pp. 412-459 in M. D. Intriligator (ed.) Frontiers of Quantitative Economics. Amsterdam: North Holland.

——— (1971b) "An econometric study of cotton production and trade, 1830-1860." Rev. of Economics and Statistics 53 (May): 111-120.

YOSHIHARA, K. (1969) "Demand functions: an application to the Japanese expenditure pattern." Econometrica 37 (April): 257-274.

The Ethnocultural Model of Voting

A Behavioral and Historical Critique

JAMES E. WRIGHT
Dartmouth College

Political action, especially individual voting choice, is a subject of major interest to contemporary behavioral scientists. They use models of political behavior to understand and explain a wide range of social tensions, roles, and attitudes. In recent years especially, historians have begun to analyze and reinterpret popular voting in an effort to understand the historical dimensions of these sociopolitical processes.

HISTORIANS AND VOTING BEHAVIOR

For most of the twentieth century, the dominant interpretation of historical political behavior has been an economic one, although Frederick Jackson Turner and his followers often used economic interests as a subset of sectional concerns. The politicization of economic conflict between propertied and unpropertied, capital and labor, "have" and "have not," not only made intuitive sense, but it made coherent the great issues which had rocked our political history: the tariff, federal land policy, railroad regulation, control of business, recognition of

[35]

the rights of labor, monetary policy, and welfare issues, to name a few. It also made sensible the political implications of industrialization, urbanization, and westward expansion—those major forces in our development as a nation (see Beard, 1957). Historians began to raise serious questions about the economic-class conflict model shortly after World War II. In a world marked by violent unrest, by authoritarian politics, and by incisive political conflict, the American experience seemed retrospectively to be serene and peaceful. Our differences, while sharply contested, did not suggest a conflict model, but rather one of consensus. Issues concerning type of government, basic economic systems, or a state church have not been generally politicized. We have agreed upon fundamentals and fought our political battles over means and programs, not philosophy (Hofstadter, 1948; Hartz, 1955).

The consensus model has fallen into disfavor in the last several years. Some younger historians began to reformulate a Beardian hypothesis that emphasized basic economic conflict (see Bernstein, 1967). Yet while they have exposed many logical and methodological fallacies in the consensus interpretation, they have not yet developed an acceptable economic framework to replace it. Part of the reason for this rests in the fact that a new school of history, that which emphasizes ethnocultural conflict in popular voting, has made a more compelling empirical case.[1]

The ethnocultural interpretation of political and social conflict has become largely synonymous with what has been called the "new political history." Historians familiar with the behavioral sciences and trained in the manipulation and analysis of large data sets have begun in recent years to rethink and rewrite much of our history. Sophisticated computer technology and social science software have played a large role in making this possible. Vast bodies of individual and aggregate data, in the form of census records, tax lists, vital statistics, church records, and election results remain a great untapped source of historical information. And this type of research has permitted us to focus on the behavior of nonelites in a manner that was virtually impossible in the study of manuscript sources. The initial—and nearly unanimous—results suggest that our historical political cleavages have been ethnic and religious, not economic.

THE ETHNOCULTURAL MODEL OF VOTING BEHAVIOR

Lee Benson (1961) and Samuel P. Hays (1965) have played key roles in the growth of the ethnocultural model. In their own writings and in their training of young historians, they have helped to shape an imaginative and persuasive approach to historical political behavior. Benson (1961: 165) perhaps described the model most concisely when he wrote that "at least since the 1820's, when manhood suffrage became widespread, ethnic and religious differences have tended to be relatively the most important sources of political differences."

Research in recent years seems to support the Benson thesis. Whether in the election of Andrew Jackson or of John Fitzgerald Kennedy, the ethnic-religious factor seems to have been a persistent determinant of political judgment and behavior (Bogue, 1968; Swierenga, 1971; McSeveney, 1971). National political debate may well have focused on economic issues such as the tariff, but community reference groups and cultural values provided the basis for electoral cleavage. Ethnocultural historians have cautioned us that these observations do not reflect a simplistic model in which ward heelers appeal to ethnic, religious, or racial prejudices and loyalties in order to divert attention from "real" economic issues. Rather, the real issues of politics have been those most significant relative to life style and values: prohibition, public funding or control of sectarian schools, sabbatarian laws, woman suffrage, and efforts to hasten or retard ethnic assimilation.

It is as it applies to the late nineteenth century (the period from the 1870s to the 1890s) that I would like to discuss the ethnocultural model of politics in some detail. This is the period in which some of the more sophisticated recent work has been done. And it is here that Richard J. Jensen (1971) and Paul Kleppner (1970), in their studies of midwestern politics have moved beyond the observation of ethnic voting patterns to the development of an ethnocultural explanation of political behavior. Their work is not unique, but is representative of scholars such as Ronald P. Formisano (1971), Lee Benson (1961), Michael F. Holt (1969), Samuel Hays (1965), John M. Allswang (1971), and Bruce M. Stave (1970), among others.[2] In addition, tangential studies by Walter Dean Burnham (1970), Frederick C. Luebke (1969), Roger E. Wyman (1968a, 1968b), and Samuel McSeveney (1972) permit an examination of the general applicability of the ethnocultural model.

For our purposes, we will define the ethnocultural interpretation of politics as one that argues that among all of the personal, interpersonal, intergroup, and intragroup factors which determine political behavior, *generally* (but not exclusively) ethnocultural grouping is the most important. This is a different perspective from a simple interest in ethnic history and politics. It posits that the ethnoreligious group was the primary determinant of political values and behavior. Paul Kleppner (1970: 35) summarized the model well:

Partisan affiliations were not rooted in economic class distinctions. They were political expressions of shared values derived from the voter's membership in, and commitment to, ethnic and religious groups. Collectively, such values provided the voter with a perspective through which he filtered existential stimuli and by means of which he translated an array of diverse events into personally relevant terms.

Clearly this is more than an observation of differential political behavior among various ethnic and religious groups. Contemporary politicians and journalists as well as later scholars have long noted this. But they have tended to dismiss it as a spurious relationship or as "irrational" behavior.

The ethnocultural historians have amassed impressive evidence to test and validate their interpretation. Further, they have developed a plausible model to explain it. Republican supporters (and in most cases Whig in the 1830s and 1840s) were the pietistic or evangelical church groups—excepting the Southerners—immigrants as well as old stock. The major Democratic constituents were the liturgical church groups, predominantly the Irish Catholics and German Catholics and Lutherans, as well as Southerners, including those transplanted into the North. Democrats had some support from non-evangelical native Protestants as well.

The ethnocultural historians have demonstrated that this relationship between religion and politics remains strong when economic factors are controlled. This challenges effectively what Samuel Hays has called the liberal (economic) interpretation of history. Richard Jensen (1971: 58) argues that "religion was the fundamental source of political conflict in the Midwest. Religion shaped the issues and the rhetoric of politics, and played the critical role in determining the party alignments of the voters."

These new behavioral historians have postulated a model which makes rational rather than chaotic the relationship between cultural group and political behavior. Religion and ethnicity are primary forces, abetted by the family, in the process of socialization. As variables in political behavior, these are significant as reference groups. But the behavioral historians go beyond simple reference group theory in the development of their model, for reference groups can be transitory and their members significantly cross-pressured. Rather, the values learned and perceptions affected by membership in an ethnic or religious group are more complex and permanent. The pietists (described in some instances as Puritans or evangelicals) were concerned with "right behavior," to use Kleppner's concise phrase. They viewed the state as a positive authority with which to regulate and direct the behavior of individuals and groups. Blue laws and prohibition were probably two of the major concerns of the pietists and the consequences of their action.

Liturgicals (or ritualists), on the other hand, stressed right belief. They were more concerned with doctrine and dogma than they were with secular behavior. Indeed, in the great battles over prohibition and sabbatarian laws, the Irish and the Germans, whether Catholic or Lutheran, provided the basis of the opposition to the pietists. Beyond this, the liturgicals placed a high value on a parochial education as a significant part of the process of socialization and religious indoctrination. They jealously and zealously protected their schools and sought public funding for these institutions. Pietists saw the schools as part of a black-robed conspiracy to resist assimilation and to raid the public funds. They insisted upon public controls over these institutions. Doctrinal differences influenced secular behavior.

To the ethnoculturalists, Wisconsin politics in the period from the 1850s to the 1890s has provided impressive validation of their model. In the period immediately prior to the Civil War, the Know-Nothing (anti-Catholic) movement and the moral issues of slavery and prohibition laid down political cleavages along ethnic and religious lines. Republican enactment of a prohibition law in 1873 and a public school law in 1890 with strong anti-Catholic and anti-foreign overtones exacerbated the old tensions. Republican gubernatorial losses following passage of these two laws (the only losses the party suffered in Wisconsin between 1854 and 1932) indicated the strength of the Germans and Catholics when aroused. Religious and doctrinal overtones existed in other campaigns, but always a good bit more subtly.

According to Kleppner and Jensen, even the major electoral realignment completed in 1896 related more to doctrinal perceptions than to William Jennings Bryan's economic and monetary proposals. In 1896, many saw Bryan as the more pietistic candidate.

It is impossible to do justice in a few pages to the cumulative decades of research and volumes of findings of the ethno-cultural historians. Suffice it to say that they have done their work well. It is virtually impossible to avoid their frame of reference in writing on American political history. Their observations are supported by statistical evidence. Their model of behavior is much more imaginative and convincing, retrospectively, than anything that has preceded it.

Yet the new ethnocultural school has not defined a universal model of historical voting behavior in the United States. Nor have these historians generally claimed to have achieved this. A behavioral approach to voting virtually rules out a monistic interpretation. In the remainder of this paper, I would like to offer a critique of the methodology and concepts employed in the approach that Richard Jensen and Paul Kleppner represent and offer some suggestions for a behavioral framework for interpreting historical voting.

METHODOLOGICAL PROBLEMS AND THE ETHNOCULTURAL MODEL

DESCRIPTION AND DEFINITION

Historians trained in modern social science techniques find it often frustrating to turn from literature rich in survey data to historical aggregations. Some individual data are available but for political historians the dependent variable, voting choice, is always in aggregate form. This causes serious methodological problems in terms of designing statistical tests and making inferences about individual behavior and causal relationships. In addition to simple correlation analyses, many of the ethno-culturalists have identified and examined clusters of aggregations, attempting to control for other variables—e.g., analyzing heavily German Lutheran units by making comparisons with clusters of units containing large numbers of pietistic Lutherans or German Catholics, and intracluster comparisons between wealthy and poor German Lutherans.

Nearly all the ethnoculturalists have used this technique of examination and inference. But they have generally not questioned the assumptions involved in using relatively homogeneous units for their observations. If our society has indeed been marked by sharp ethnocultural conflict, then homogeneous communities might not be microcosms for the analysis of the behavioral implications of these tensions. Further, one might question the use of "German Lutheran" or any such description without reference to time and place. This fails to control for differential levels of acculturation as a function of quantitative (as well as qualitative) relationships with the dominant culture. Clearly Luebke's (1969: 35) impressive work in Nebraska demonstrates that cultural "mix" was important, but without minimizing the overall influence of religion:

> If the mixed immigrant community was small, establishing social and religious institutions on an ethnic basis was difficult. Unless the German was a resident of a ghetto, he was forced to mingle with the dominant native American stock, which greatly increased the tendency to conform to majority standards.

In a recently published study, Samuel McSeveney (1972) found ethnocultural factors quite significant in voting in New York, New Jersey, and Connecticut in the 1890s, but modified, at times considerably, by factionalism, localism, and personalities.

The use of homogeneous communities, of course, opens a further question of definition. The ethnoculturalists are not generally precise in defining a "largely German" town. Kleppner (1970: 21, 23), for example, refers to units that are the "most heavily Catholic" in the city, that are a "stronghold of German Lutherans," and are "working class," but without giving a measurement for the specific cases in these descriptive categories. Obviously, relative is the operational term here. Of Jensen's (1971: 142) Wisconsin "German" units, an examination of the 1895 Wisconsin state census reveals that Wheatland had 26% German natives, Randall had 24%, and Lomira 27%. His Iowa German counties were those in which over 10% of the 1900 population was German-born (Jensen, 1971: 96, n. 14). There would, of course, be second- and third-generation Germans in these towns as well, but literature on ethnic acculturation, while conceding the persistence of ethnic ties, would generally caution us against treating such individuals as culturally monolithic (see discussion in Luebke, 1969: 40-41, ch. 3 and throughout).

A corollary question that faces all students of voting behavior, but might be raised in the context of selection of representative units, involves levels of participation. This is particularly crucial in the analysis of still-acculturating immigrant groups. If a civil unit is composed of two-thirds Germans this obviously does not mean that two-thirds of the voters are Germans. Kleppner, for example, analyzes the French Canadian vote in Michigan and Wisconsin by looking at "French Canadian lumbering" units. Yet, in New England at any rate, French Canadians were characterized by extremely low levels of political participation. As late as the 1930s one-third of the French Canadians (and 38% of the Italians) in Burlington, Vermont, never voted (Anderson, 1937: 207-210). Similar evidence of low levels of participation exists for towns in New Hampshire and Connecticut in the late nineteenth and early twentieth centuries (Bourassa, 1972; McSeveney, 1972: 125). In characterizing civil units, "Who voted?" is a more critical question—if a more elusive answer—than "What were the general population profiles?"

THE RELIGIOUS VARIABLE

Religion is a more crucial variable in the ethnocultural model than is national stock. It is religion that provides the key to descriptions of differential behavior and the interpretive framework to understand it. Yet there are methodological problems in defining religious characteristics. Religion was not a universal characteristic of the population. Religious sociologists differ on measurement of religiosity, but clearly they would agree that church membership is not the only measurement of a religious person (see, for example, Glock and Stark, 1965: ch. 2; Yinger, 1970: 24-32). It remains, however, the only objectively verifiable one for historical aggregates. Both Jensen and Kleppner have attempted to make meaningful the figures on religious communicants. Kleppner (1970: 99) has estimated that the increase in membership in major religious groups from 1870 to 1890 was from 65% to 75% of the population in

Michigan, from 75% to 85% in Ohio, and from 60% to 85% in Wisconsin. Jensen (1971: 85-88) has estimated that, in 1890, 73% of the population of the Midwest belonged to a church. My own estimates for the religious population of Wisconsin and Iowa in 1890, using the federal census of religious bodies and population over fifteen years of age as the base, are 52% and 46%, respectively. Clearly, this does not mean that the balance of the population was irreligious or atheist. Probably few were. Yet, as we shall see later, this methodological problem of description can lead to a broader conceptual problem of definition.

Richard Jensen has made a major effort to break down voting aggregates by locating and analyzing contemporary directories that list occupation, religion and political preferences for individuals. In these compilations, he demonstrates that few of those individuals who belonged to old stock, pietistic churches described themselves as Democrats, while the Catholics were predominantly Democratic. Nonpietistic Protestants were found between these two extremes.

Jensen's individual analyses underline the earlier questions about religion. Only 43% of one group and 50% of the other expressed a religious preference. This is of some significance in light of the commercial nature of these publications: non-membership must have been socially acceptable.

RELIGION AND CLASS

The Jensen tabulations are relevant to a major methodological question concerning the ethnocultural school: have they adequately controlled for class? Or, correlatively, have they satisfactorily demonstrated that there has been no relationship between religion and class? Jensen's compilation for eight Illinois townships, for example, shows that, among liturgicals, 25.2% were involved in business, professional, and white-collar occupations, as opposed to 42.5% of the pietists. More significantly, 46.9% of the liturgicals were unskilled laborers, as compared to 14.1% of the pietists. These data

would indicate some relationship between religion and occupation. And, indeed, the liturgicals, especially the Roman
Catholics, were largely recent immigrants who moved to the
cities and took low-paying, low-status jobs. There are no general
data on religion and occupation, but census tabulations for
1890 linking ethnicity and occupation are revealing (U.S.
Department of the Interior, Census Office, 1897). For example,
native white of native parents composed 62.49% of the white
population in 1890; foreign-born whites were 16.59%. Yet the
immigrants composed 43.41% of the common laborers and the
native stock group composed 41.26%. As the ethnoculturalists
have properly warned us, however, the immigrant community
should not be treated as a monolith. A ranking among major
immigrant groups using percentage of that group working as
laborers shows that 34.15% of the Italians in 1890 were
laborers, followed by Hungarians (32.44%), Irish (25.16%),
French Canadians (16.43%), Bohemians (15.90%), Swedes and
Norwegians (14.95%), Danes (13.30%), Germans (11.58%),
Russians (10.96%), and various British groups at ten percent or
less. Significantly, the groups with the highest proportion of
their members working as laborers tended to be liturgical in
religious doctrine. Of course, many of the groups listed here had
but recently arrived in 1890, and it should not be too surprising
that new immigrants began as laborers. Beyond this, cultural
heritage does affect occupational choice (or option) in ways not
directly related to employment discrimination. Yet these
complex qualifications do not affect the basic relationship
between job status and nativity. The Irish were not recent
arrivals. They were among the earliest of the major immigrant
groups and, among second-generation Irishmen, laborer was still
the most common occupation. Some 17.88% of the native-born
with Irish mothers were laborers (there were no compilations on
native-born with Irish fathers) This compared with 8.51% of
the overall second-generation group. French Canadians and
Italians showed equally minimal generational mobility.

Obviously, these general figures are not conclusive of
anything. Yet they do suggest a relationship between occu-

pation and ethnicity that must be investigated further before we can completely rule out occupational class as an intervening or contributing variable in the ethnocultural model of political behavior. Indeed, Robert Hodge and Donald Tremain (1968) recently demonstrated that even subjective class perceptions are influenced by nonoccupational associations.

CONCEPTUAL PROBLEMS AND THE ETHNOCULTURAL MODEL

THE COMPLEXITY OF CULTURE

Beyond these general methodological problems, the ethnocultural interpretation also raises some conceptual questions. For example, the ethnocultural historians generally treat religion and ethnicity as unidimensional concepts, without reference to time, place, rate of acculturation, or individual personality. The latter two are elusive, admittedly, for which historical variables would be extremely difficult to generate. Nevertheless, we must recognize that ethnicity is part of an interactive social system and while significant it is by no means universally dominant. The Irish Catholic immigrant living in a solidly Irish ward in Boston in 1900 would relate to his ethnicity in different ways than he would if he found himself living in an exclusive Brahmin section—and in different ways yet if he moved to a French Canadian mill town or to an old stock but poor pietistic farming community in Vermont. Environment is a crucial variable in behavior. Society is not static, nor are the perceptions and relationships which shape it. McSeveney (1972: 226) found, for example, that Germans and evangelical Protestants voted similarly in New Jersey in 1893. Perhaps most significantly, they voted Democratic in Atlantic County and Republican elsewhere. And the dominant issue (racetracks) was a "moral" one, apparently eliciting neither a strictly doctrinal nor a uniform partisan response.

Ethnicity cannot be conceptualized as the dominant variable

in all social relationships. It is not a singular characteristic. The ethnoculturalists concede this when they point to the "deviant" South, in which the dominant, old-stock white pietists were overwhelmingly Democratic. Racial tensions and prejudices obviously influenced this development. But there might well be other exceptions to the ethnocultural rule. For example, more work needs to be done on the election of 1896 before we can describe it as supportive of the ethnocultural model. Those pietistic farmers who supported Bryan in 1896 may have done so because his evangelical style appealed to their sense of "right behavior." Jensen (1971: 270) argued, for example, "In the spring and summer of 1896 the silverite monetary doctrines captured the imagination and excited the utopian longings of pietistic midwestern farmers" (see also Kleppner, 1970: 338-368). Yet these voters might also have responded to Bryan as farmers, and their pietism may have been a supportive—or irrelevant—factor. Roger Wyman (1968b) found economic forces—not class—significant in the Wisconsin realignment, but conditioned by politicoreligious traditions.

RELIGIOUS DOCTRINE AND INDIVIDUAL BEHAVIOR

The ethnocultural historians have not adequately defined the model whereby doctrinal predilections, abetted by religious cues, have measureable behavioral implications. The model is at once too simple and incomplete: A basic religious frame of reference and value hierarchy interpreting diverse stimuli and information and relating them to the dominant (pietist/ liturgical) values, with predictable behavior patterns. We might well remember religious sociologist J. Milton Yinger's (1970: 455) conclusion in dealing with the relationship between religious fundamentalism and right-wing politics:

> Fundamentalist religion does not "cause" reactionary politics any more than hydrogen "causes" sugar, regardless of the availability of carbon and oxygen. It may, if present in the right amounts, and under particular conditions, be part of a compound. But in different situations, other compounds are formed.

Few contemporary religious sociologists would qualify this statement. Religion is significant, but seldom dominant. And we have no hard evidence to indicate otherwise historically. Indeed, the low levels of religious membership discussed earlier calls into question the process by which nonmembers receive the requisite stimuli. For example, Gerhard Lenski (1961: 174-179) and Philip Converse et al. (1961) have discovered, respectively, differences in political attitude and behavior between communicants and noncommunicants. As Jensen, Kleppner, and others have convincingly demonstrated, the stimuli were present in various forms in the period extending from the 1830s into the twentieth century. But they failed to define the process by which a non-church member living in a heterogeneous community (a much more common type than the ethnoculturalists imply) receive all the stimuli. We do not know the types of cues that he was given—and by whom—to relate these stimuli to his value hierarchy and to interpret this relationship against the political options. The ethnoculturalists have inferred a good bit about this process from the election results—politicians seeking the ethnic vote and members of ethnoreligious groups transforming these appeals into relevant data—but the method remains unclear. Kleppner's (1970: 249) warning about relating the 1893 depression to political behavior might well be considered in relation to the ethnocultural interpretation: "Certainly not all voters, and probably not even a very large proportion of them, perceived the subtle and complex inter-relationships between the advent of the depression and the alternatives of public policy."

The question of stimuli-response cannot be answered simply by demonstrating the existence of doctrinal differences and the presence of politicoreligious stimuli. Their salience *relative* to other stimuli is the critical problem. How does the old-stock, pietistic Wisconsin farmer arrange and rank stimuli and values if he perceives the Democratic candidate as the candidate of Rum and Romanism and the Republican candidate as a representative of the tariff policy that caused the bottom to fall out of the Chicago hog market? And the latter, it could be asserted, has been a condition at least as common historically as politico-religious tensions. In addition, we must explicitly recognize the influence of traditional party allegiance on individual voting choice. This might well be an independent, conditioning force that transcends immediate options and "rational" choices.

Herbert George, a Colorado newspaper editor who was a sometime Populist and a notorious anti-Catholic, observed in 1896 that he "would vote for the pope of Rome if we knew him to be right on the money question and we are no Catholic sympathizer either" (Wright, 1969: 397). Without this explicit statement, it might make intuitive sense to interpret George's shift from his earlier Republicanism to support for Bryan in 1896 as a politicoreligious response to Bryan's evangelism. Yinger (1970: 205) observed that, in such a model, "Values are sometimes used to explain behavior, having themselves been inferred from examination of behavior. Until this problem is solved, values should be treated as descriptive terms, not explanatory variables."

ETHNOCULTURAL FACTORS AND STATUS

Finally, and perhaps most importantly, the ethnoculturalists have failed to consider the relationship between ethnoreligious groups and status. They have attempted to control for class but have virtually neglected the more comprehensive concept of status. It might be argued that the latter is more relevant to the American experience. As indicated earlier, the linkage between ethnoreligious factors and class may indeed be significant. But there may be even more universal and persistent linkage with status. Controlling for the wealth of civil units and the occupation of individuals inadequately deals with this problem. Michael Parenti's (1967: 723) conclusions are relevant:

> Even if full social acceptance is won without serious encounters with bigotry, it is unlikely that from childhood to adulthood one will have escaped a realization that some kind of stigma is attached to one's minority identity, that one is in some way "marginal." Ethnic identifications are, after all, rarely neutral.

The evidence would suggest that, in the nineteenth century, "full social acceptance" would be exceptional. It would seem a reasonable hypothesis that the Catholic immigrant groups (excepting possibly the Germans in some areas) generally in the nineteenth century ranked near the bottom of the status hierarchy, regardless of economic success. In his study of "Paper City," Kenneth Underwood (1957: 191) observed that

> Objective data of occupation, income and place of residence may place some Protestants and Roman Catholics in the same economic class, but subjective data such as "consciousness of kind" and degree of esteem evidenced in visiting and freely associating in activities with one another, dating with intent to marry, reveal cleavages based on religion and nationality.

The consequence of mobility for many ethnics was status inconsistency (see Knoke, 1972). This is a difficult factor to isolate relative to the ethnocultural model of political behavior. The persistent Democratic voting of a successful Irish businessman may have been the product of either a transcendent doctrinal orientation or it may have resulted from his experience with a Republican status hierarchy that refused to acknowledge his success and accept his mobility. The behavioral pattern (Democratic voting) would be the same in both cases, and ethnicity would be salient in each. Yet the one model would stress doctrinal forces as primary agents and the other would emphasize status.

H. Richard Niebuhr (1929: 25) asserted that religious denominations are sociological groups that, in addition to their religious functions, "represent the accommodation of religion to the caste system." Clearly this is too strong for the general American system, but it might be reformulated to suggest that historically our status system has rested to a large degree on religion and ethnicity. Case studies of blacks, Chicanos, Orientals, Jews, Irish, and eastern and southern European Catholics would seem to support this. Northern Europeans, largely Protestant, encountered fewer barriers to assimilation, and their religion was clearly a factor in this. Anti-Catholicism historically has been more that a pietist versus ritualist conflict. Witness the strong anti-Catholicism of German Lutherans.

Richard Jensen's data show occupational differentiation between pietists and liturgicals. He infers from this that job discrimination may have existed on political grounds. The liturgicals tended to be Democrats and the pietists Republicans. But, he concludes (Jensen, 1971: 314-315), "There is no evidence of it [job discrimination] on religious grounds." This seems a rather tenuous cause-and-effect relationship that indeed runs counter to the ethnoculturalists' emphasis on the saliency of religion.

BEHAVIORALISM AND HISTORICAL VOTING

Despite these criticisms of their methodological approach and conceptual framework, the fact remains that the ethnocultural historians have immeasurably raised our levels of knowledge and understanding of the processes of historical voting behavior. They have forced us to confront religious differences and ethnic tensions as a significant political force. They have broadened our framework to include local issues as salient components of political debate and cleavage. Their religious-doctrinal-theological interpretation of observations of ethnoreligious voting has been the basis of these criticisms rather than the observations themselves. Seymour Lipset (1964: 72) observed several years ago that four variables influenced "the basic political differentiation among American religious bodies." These were (1) social status, (2) economic class, (3) anti-Catholicism "in both its religious and ethnic form," and (4) the "level of concern with 'public morality.'" The ethnoculturalists generally have focused on the last variable to the exclusion of the other three.

Behavioral scientists have liberated us from the need to search for "the" interpretation of voting. Behavior is too complex for neat categorization, easy description, or generalization. In the study of voting, we must first of all differentiate between the individual and the group. The latter is discrete by definition, homogeneous in composition, and usually unitary in function and behavior. Thus the group "Methodists" is composed of members (formal or informal) of the Methodist church, deals with doctrinal, administrative, and social problems of Methodism, and behaves as Methodists. An *individual Methodist,* however, has a variety of other roles that he may play: e.g., carpenter, homeowner, mortgagor, father, urbanite, German native, and member of the Grand Army of the Republic, the Masons, the Knights Templar, and a building trades union. These and other roles and statuses may independently or collectively affect his behavior, depending on issue saliency, perceptions, and cognitions (for an essential agreement, see Kleppner, 1970: 100-101, 120). Further, as Robert Merton (1957: 233) has suggested, groups to which an individual does not belong are likewise relevant to his perceptions and behavior. Beyond this, we must distinguish between associational and communal membership.[3] The latter is informal and not easily defined but, as Lenski (1961: 157-165) observed, it has greater behavioral implications. So while "Methodism" is analytically convenient—and at times a crucial predictor of behavior—it as as limited as "working class" in its usefulness. Religious association is part of a vast matrix of individual memberships and roles.[4] The high correlation of religion with voting does not mean that we should assume a causal relationship or infer a doctrinal source of individual motivation. In Colorado, ethnicity was a high correlate of political behavior in the 1880s and 1890s. Yet multivariate analysis reveals an economic rather than cultural saliency after 1890 (Wright, 1969).

The preliminary findings of my research into New Hampshire politics indicate that, in the 1880s, towns dominated by the Freewill Baptists or by the Methodists were largely Democratic, while the Congregational towns were Republican. All three religious groups tended to be pietistic, but the Freewill Baptists were the most pietistic—and, apparently, the most Democratic.

A doctrinal interpretation of this behavior is not consistent with the observation, but it is true that the Congregationalists represented historically the religious establishment in the state while the others were the progeny of the dissenters. A complex of tradition, status, religion, and economics seemed to influence behavior. With regard to the latter, it is revealing that it was virtually impossible to locate "poor" Congregational communities and "wealthy" Freewill Baptist communities. It might be suggested that, in the Midwest, these three groups all tended to be more "establishment" and enjoyed higher status than the Catholic immigrants.

Conversely, it appears that, among the liturgicals in New Hampshire, the Irish were overwhelmingly Democratic and the French Canadians, when voting, marginally so, with occasional support for the Republican Party. This can best be understood by a study of the sharp conflicts between these two groups over control of the church hierarchy and over the language to be used in the various parishes. The Irish were more acculturated than the French Canadians and probably served more often as foremen in the mills. Religion was a factor in this behavior. Doctine was not; or, at the most, it was minimally so.

As Yinger (1970: 456) put it,

> Knowledge of religious training, membership, or expressed belief by itself yields relatively little power to predict political attitudes and behavior. Knowledge of the structural context, non-religious cultural elements in the environment, and a wide range of individual tendencies is needed before we can state what the implications of given religious forces are.

In short, we must know more about broad social and institutional configurations before we can construct a behavioral model of historical voting. The ethnocultural historians have taken us a major step in that direction. The journey is by no means over.

NOTES

1. The differences here may often be more apparent than real. Benson (1961), for example, essentially agrees with the consensus approach, while stressing ethnoreligious conflict. I think it fair to say that few of the ethnoculturalists explicitly embrace the consensus framework.

2. I have chosen to focus on Jensen and Kleppner because their work together represents the most extensive effort to develop a model of voting behavior and because this permits a somewhat fixed reference point for my discussion. I do not mean to imply that their work is necessarily better—and certainly not weaker—than the other ethnocultural studies. I do think that their work has probably captured more attention among historians than that of the other ethnoculturalists, excepting Benson and Hays. And it must be recognized—and admitted—that it is difficult to generalize about such a diverse, rich body of literature. Certainly the criticisms which make up the bulk of this paper are not equally applicable to all these historians, nor, in all cases, even to Jensen and Kleppner who freely concede the complexity of the problem. My comments instead focus on general themes and central tendencies.

3. Ferdinand Tonnies clarified this distinction, and both Weber and Durkheim made analytical use of it. For a brief discussion, see Lenski (1961: 19).

4. A significant factor in the development of the ethnocultural school is the pluralist interpretation of political and social relations. Often the two are used synonymously (Swierenga, 1971: 67). I regret not having space to examine this relationship here. Suffice it to say that the ethnocultural interpretation has not developed a matrix of groups but rather has substituted vertical social cleavages for horizontal ones. Further, their model operationally defines a dichotomous politics (pietist versus liturgical) rather than a pluralist one (see Yinger, 1970: 425-430, esp. illustration on 426). His "columnar model" coincides with the ethnocultural one (see also Gordon, 1964: 42-51).

REFERENCES

ALLSWANG, J. M. (1971) A House for All Peoples: Ethnic Politics in Chicago, 1890-1936. Lexington: Univ. of Kentucky Press.
ANDERSON, E. L. (1937) We Americans: A Study of Cleavage in an American City. Cambridge, Mass.: Harvard Univ. Press.
BEARD, W. [comp.] (1957) The Economic Basis of Politics and Related Writings by Charles Beard. New York: Vintage.
BENSON, L. (1961) The Concept of Jacksonian Democracy: New York as a Test Case. Princeton: Princeton Univ. Press.
BERNSTEIN, B. J. (1967) Towards a New Past: Dissenting Essays in American History. New York: Random House.
BOGUE, A. G. (1968) "United States: the 'new' political history." J. of Contemporary History 3 (January): 5-25.

BOURASSA, D. C. (1972) "Franco-Americans in Manchester." Dartmouth College. (unpublished)

BURNHAM, W. D. (1970) Critical Elections and the Mainsprings of American Politics. New York: W. W. Norton.

CONVERSE, P. E., A. CAMPBELL, W. E. MILLER, and D. E. STOKES (1961) "Stability and change in 1960: a reinstating election." Amer. Pol. Sci. Rev. 55 (June): 269-280.

FORMISANO, R. P. (1971) The Birth of Mass Political Parties: Michigan, 1827-1861. Princton: Princeton Univ. Press.

GLOCK, C. Y. and R. STARK (1965) Religion and Society in Tension. Chicago: Rand McNally.

GORDON, M. M. (1964) Assimilation in American Life: The Role of Race, Religion and National Origins. New York: Oxford Univ. Press.

HARTZ, L. (1955) The Liberal Tradition in America. New York: Harcourt, Brace & World.

HAYS, S. P. (1965) "The social analysis of American political history." Pol. Sci. Q. 80: 373-394.

HODGE, R. W. and D. J. TREMAIN (1968) "Class identification in the United States." Amer. J. of Sociology 73 (March): 535-547.

HOFSTADTER, R. (1948) The American Political Tradition. New York: Alfred A. Knopf.

HOLT, M. F. (1969) Forging a Majority: The Formation of the Republican Party in Pittsburgh, 1848-1860. New Haven, Conn.: Yale Univ. Press.

JENSEN, R. J. (1971) The Winning of the Midwest: Social and Political Conflict, 1888-1896. Chicago: Univ. of Chicago Press.

KLEPPNER, P. (1970) The Cross of Culture: A Social Analysis of Midwestern Politics, 1850-1900. New York: Free Press.

KNOKE, D. (1972) "Community and consistency: the ethnic factor in status inconsistency." Social Forces 51 (September): 23-33.

LENSKI, G. (1961) The Religious Factor: A Sociological Study of Religion's Impact on Politics, Economics, and Family Life. Garden City, N.Y.: Doubleday.

LIPSET, S. M. (1964) "Religion and politics in the American past and present," pp. 69-126 in R. Lee and M. E. Marty (eds.) Religion and Social Conflict. New York: Oxford Univ. Press.

LUEBKE, F. C. (1969) Immigrants and Politics: The Germans of Nebraska, 1880-1900. Lincoln: Univ. of Nebraska.

McSEVENEY, S. T. (1972) The Politics of Depression: Political Behavior in the Northeast, 1893-1896. New York: Oxford Univ. Press.

––– (1971) "Ethnic groups, ethnic conflicts, and recent quantitative research in American political history." (unpublished)

MERTON, R. (1957) Social Theory and Social Structure. New York: Free Press.

NIEBUHR, H. R. (1929) The Social Sources of Denominationalism. New York: Henry Holt.

PARENTI, M. (1967) "Ethnic politics and the persistence of ethnic identification." Amer. Pol. Sci. Rev. 61 (September): 717-726.

STAVE, B. M. (1970) The New Deal and the Last Hurrah: Pittsburgh Machine Politics. Pittsburgh: Univ. of Pittsburgh Press.

SWIERENGA, R. P. (1971) "Ethnocultural political analysis: a new approach to American ethnic studies." J. of Amer. Studies 5 (April): 59-79.

UNDERWOOD, K. W. (1957) Protestant and Catholic: Religious and Social Interaction in an Industrial Community. Boston: Beacon.

U.S. Department of the Interior, Census Office (1897) Report on Population of the United States at the Eleventh Census: 1890. Washington: Government Printing Office.

WRIGHT, J. E. (1969) "The politics of populism: parties, partisans and dissenters in Colorado, 1860-1912." Ph.D. dissertation. University of Wisconsin.

WYMAN, R. E. (1968a) "Wisconsin ethnic groups and the election of 1890." Wisconsin Magazine of History 51 (Summer): 269-293.

——— (1968b) "Voter realignment in Wisconsin in the 1890's." Presented to the Wisconsin Association of Teachers of College History, October.

YINGER, J. M. (1970) The Scientific Study of Religion. New York: Macmillan.

American Legislative Behavior

ROBERT ZEMSKY
University of Pennsylvania

Legislative history once belonged to the parliamentarians, a small band of aficionados whose carefully wrought studies were read by each other and almost no one else. To most historians, the legislative process and its constitutional development was not a matter of concern. Political history dealt with men and events and great issues and decidedly not with the texture of institutional life in America. Then, in the 1960s, the discovery of a core of behavioral theory detailing how political decisions are now made, encouraged a number of historians to look again at the American Congress. Primarily interested in the Civil War and Reconstruction, these historians argued that behavior-based legislative theories and accompanying statistical models would supply new answers to a host of questions which had divided the historical craft. When did sectionalism emerge as the dominant force in America? When and how was the Whig Party destroyed? Who were the radicals who gave Reconstruction its peculiar cast?

In part, the new legislative history also reflected a rekindled interest in the quantification of historical data and hence the belief that counting could control the historian's traditional biases. Again the behavioral sciences supplied technique, rationale, and encouragement. Those who questioned the applicability of statistics in a historical setting were treated as troglodytes, as men committed to a bygone era and outmoded values. To those who remained merely skeptical, the quantifier had but one response: "The proof will be in the pudding."

In 1967 appeared the first major legislative studies cast in the new mold, Joel Silbey (1967) and Thomas Alexander (1967). As promised, a statistics-based roll call analysis identified the ebb and flow of legislative alliances. The interplay between sectional interest and party loyalty was sketched in new detail, as was the inexorable demise of the Whig Party as a prelude to the Civil War. Two thoughtful and careful historians had aptly demonstrated that political science methodology could in fact enrich the historical imagination.

Their larger achievement, however, lies in the questions their studies occasion. Although each study used similar techniques to analyze identical roll call sets, they offered quite different interpretations of the central forces at work in the antebellum Congress. Silbey contended that party organization, not sectional loyalty, governed congressional behavior in the 1840s. Alexander agreed, but then went on to document that underlying party cohesion was a strong tide of sectional stress which eventually engulfed the legislative arena. The skeptics chortled. Quantification had contributed but one more fruitless round in the seemingly endless debate over the role of sectionalism in American history.

More important, perhaps, Silbey and Alexander implicitly suggest the price one pays in borrowing someone else's methodology. Both studies exist in a curious vacuum, as though the only business of Congress was to supply future historians with roll call data with which to reconstruct our political past. Nor did either study ask, "Did roll calls in the 1840s perform the same function as they do today?" For political scientists, roll call analysis is essentially a descriptive technique (Price, 1963). While comparative studies tracing political alliances over time did not interest the political scientist, longitudinal analysis dominated Alexander and Silbey's studies, as both sought the rate at which sectional interests destroyed party loyalties. No less, they sought to measure the changing salience of a set of predetermined issues in each Congress, asking when slavery became a central issue of sufficient divisiveness to break down party loyalties.

Of the two studies, Alexander's dealt more directly with the problems of longitudinal analysis. Indeed, he and Silbey reached different conclusions precisely because Alexander employed the more robust research design. Alexander's methodology identified changes which cropped up first in one regional section of one party and then spilled over into other sections and eventually into the other party until the entire structure of voting was transformed. Silbey was right when he argued that, at any given moment during the 1840s, party was a better predictor than section of a vote's outcome. What went undetected, however, was the magnitude, rate, and loci of specific changes in voting patterns.

While Alexander was able to isolate the more subtle changes in voting behavior, he, like Silbey, blurred over a second obstacle to longitudinal analysis. Each study relied on Guttman scaling to identify clusters of related roll calls and issue dimensions (such as slavery) within a given Congress. And each asked if particular congressmen from specific regions and parties changed their positions over time. Did they become more or less moderate or radical as issues became more salient and potentially more divisive? To answer such questions, Alexander and Silbey assumed that a moderate score on the "slavery" scale in the Twenty-Sixth Congress was roughly the same as a moderate score on "slavery" in the Twenty-Seventh Congress. In fact, we have little reason to assume such comparability. Where one Congress may focus on a narrow range of slavery issues, its successor may extend its purview and increase the probability of divisions. Conceivably a specific resolution could be considered radical in one context and moderate in another, if in the later Congress, new, even more radical resolutions were introduced. Thus a congressman could have seemingly adopted a radical stance in the Twenty-Sixth Congress and a moderate position in the Twenty-Seventh Congress without changing his attitude toward the regulation of slavery. More is involved here than technique, though the argument is often mired in technicalities. In part, the historian's interest in the behavioral sciences bespeaks a certain fadishness, a desire to be au courant, to assimilate into our conception of a unique past the present's preoccupation with a general theory of human behavior and its promise of social amelioration. But we have also become believers. Despite ritualistic skepticism, we have assumed that behavioral theory enriches the historical imagination by providing a framework for interpretive argument. To the extent that we resist speaking of self-evident truths buried amid mounds of computer print-out, we also preserve our belief in a unique past, one determined by a particular conjunction of time and space. With perhaps misplaced pugnacity, Silbey spoke for most behavioral historians when, at the end of his study, he outlined the kind of political history we ought to be writing:

> The tenacity with which American congressmen clung to the national political divisions in the 1840's suggests the need for a deeper understanding of how people actually act in politics and how they react to new behavioral influences and changes in the context of political activity. Our comprehension of antebellum political processes has perhaps been wrongly shaped by what I have elsewhere referred to as "the Civil War synthesis" in our historiography. It is obvious, it seems to me, that more detailed study of all levels of American politics, without preconceived notions about the period and without primary reliance on potentially contradictory and misleading evidence, are necessary before we can fully comprehend the antebellum political scene. And, lest we repeat earlier mistakes and misplace emphases such studies should utilize, as has been done here, recent advances in statistical methodology and in our knowledge of how and why human beings act as they do.

Who shall supply that theory which Silbey believes is central to a behavioral approach to the past? Historians have assumed that the behavioral sciences would provide both theory and method. Indeed, behavioral historians have largely foresworn a creative interest in theory, in part out of deference to (if not in awe of) the rich accomplishments of the behavioral sciences, and in part because we have accepted the behavioralist's contention that a unique, physically remote past creates insurmountable obstacles to the formation of theoretical propositions of general applicability. Given the ineluctable dependence of method upon theory, we have been similarly content to adopt, and occasionally adapt, the statistical methods of the relevant behavioral sciences.

It is difficult to quarrel with such an approach. By the early 1960s, when historians first developed a sustained interest in statistics and behavioral theory, the transformation of the social sciences was all but complete. By the end of the decade, legislative analysts had extended their domain across the Atlantic, linking up with like-minded colleagues in Europe in a series of joint projects designed to yield a general theory of legislative behavior. Legislative analysts developed a variety of new, largely quantified methods for processing the volumes of data at their disposal. Roll call analysis became a subspecialty of its own. Models were built to describe power distributions, voting alliances, attitudinal clusters, and decision flows. With understandable zeal, our friends in political science hawked their newfound wares to a small but enthusiastic group of historians. After all, an election was an election just as a roll call was a roll call—both could be reduced to a statistical format and then processed by the appropriate computer routine. It was all so easy. Canned computer programs were readily avialable. Our lack of statistical expertise would prove no obstacle since, we were told, technical arguments were only for the cognescenti and really did not matter anyway. Moreover, the data were already available. The Interuniversity Consortium for Political Research had reduced to machine-readable form every roll call in the U.S. Congress since 1790 and every presidential, gubernatorial, and congressional election since 1824. Finally, there was always the implicit concern that if the historian either could or would not develop an interest in behavioral theory and quantitative techniques, the behavioral sciences would expand their empire, making the past an integral part of their own concerns. Self-interest demanded we take immediate advantage of the opportunity to recast historical methodology.

In sum, the historian's willingness to eschew theories and methods of his own invention was as understandable as it was inevitable. The early successes of the behavioral sciences, the obvious analogue between some forms of present and past data, a sense of insecurity when confronted with the confidence (and not infrequently the blandishments) of our brethren in the behavioral sciences all combined to make the borrowing of theory and method an attractive short cut to immediate progress. If we were adaptable, if we could accept on faith the pioneering efforts of others, we could gain crucial advantage over those who claimed that the statistical manipulation of numbers could only distort the historian's calling.

It is clearer now the price we paid for this act of faith. Behavioral theory is not like a historical archive: its contents cannot be searched, catalogued, or neatly filed away. It is not inert. Nor is it devoid of context. Nor for that matter, does theory exist independently from the theoretician, for all who use theory in fact become theoreticians. Theory cannot be used simply to enrich our imaginations, to suggest constructs and patterns with which to bring meaning to our data and lend strength to our interpretive arguments. For theory to perform these functions, it must be adapted to a particular context, and that process of adaptation in itself creates new theories while simultaneously defining new problems.

On a superficial level, our theoretical naivete has resulted in a series of minor embarrassments. Frequently we borrow out of context. Too often we combine competing, even contradictory theories. In general, we ignore the technical limitations a particular theory imposes simply because we do not understand how the theory was constructed. Our disinterest in theory per se has also made us a curiously captive audience. Because we remain the consumers of their theoretical wares, we tend to investigate only those situations modern behaviorists find absorbing. We have segmented the past so as to mirror the present as each of us has developed a secondary loyalty to the particular branch of behavioral science from which we borrow our specific theories and methods. Because we remain a captive audience, we have also forgotten that past and present do often require quite different approaches.

To be sure, some have recognized our dilemma. A half-dozen years ago, C. Vann Woodward (1965: 44) remarked:

> The sciences seek out the general, the abstract, the repetitive, while history rejoices in the particular, the concrete, the unique. Fundamentally, the historian feels that he is past-minded, time conscious, humanistic in spirit, skeptical in outlook. . . . He doubts that the most important problems are amenable to quantitative analysis and suspects that the social scientists pick problems their methods will solve and neglect others.

Behavioralists and traditionalists do focus on different problems, in part, as Woodward suggests, because their methods differ, and in part because each group, in ways Woodward only hints at, conceives its task in such a way as to make a genuine meld between the two perspectives extremely difficult.

A principal source of this difficulty derives from an assumption basic to all behavioral research: the assumption that researcher and subject share identical time and space. What the behavioral sciences study are responses produced by known subjects responding to stimuli observed by the researcher. While historians have understood that behavioral research involves the analysis of visible phenomena, the implication of drawing on a science of visibles to explore a now invisible past has too often been reduced to the assertion that if only the historian could interview the dead, then the methods and concerns of the behavioral sciences would become immediately relevant.

Much of the analytic confusion over roll call analysis derives from this disjunction between a visible present and an invisible past. When Price asked whether Southern Democrats were different, he already had a crucial part of the answer. In fact, the idiosyncrasies of the Southern Democracy were an ingrained part of his political culture. In general, modern behavioralists proceed in this fashion, establishing the credibility of their methods by first analyzing known outcomes. If Guttman scaling could successfully identify the South's known sensitivities on the issues of race and states rights, then probably scalograms could also detail other, less-well-perceived patterns, such as issues dealing with foreign trade.

Scale analysis is essentially a statistical routine first developed to process psychological tests. Because they are ordinarily given at one sitting, the particular order of questions does not matter. Roll calls, on the other hand, are sequential events. Intuitively, at least, their order is crucial if the legislative process is conceived of as a decision flow during which legislators record their momentary opinion on a particular piece of legislation. At first glance, then, scale analysis appears to be an inappropriate procedure for processing roll call votes. Yet, in a large number of studies dealing with modern legislatures, it has clearly worked, identifying predicted as well as meaningful clusters of related roll calls. As a minimum, then, we can assume that in most modern legislatures opinions are stable enough to allow the formation of persistent attitudes toward most legislative issues.

Perhaps congressional voting in the nineteenth century was equally stable. An individual congressman may have come to Washington with a set of well-defined attitudes so that on any given vote his mental calculus told him whether to answer yea or nay or to abstain. But this raises a question to which there is no answer. How do we establish the scalogram's credibility within a historical context? Where is the obvious test case with a known outcome? *If* we knew that sectional jealousies in the 1840s eroded party loyalties and *if* our scalograms neatly confirmed the expected patterns of behavior, *then* we too could accept Guttman scaling as a credible tool for identifying less-well-known and even unexpected voting patterns in the antebellum Congresses. Actually scale analysis presents us with a dual problem. On the one hand, scalograms make assumptions about historical voting patterns we cannot substantiate. On the other hand, scale analysis is not amenable to adjustment. The procedure simply, though rather elegantly, identifies a set of related stimuli (here, roll calls) in terms of a coherent pattern of responses. The statistical routine derives from, rather than adjusts, our theorem defining the stability of attitudes. Even if we were more competent theorists as well as statisticians, it is doubtful we could overcome the methodological and epistemological problems scale analysis poses.

Though the lesson is perhaps a painful one, our initial preoccupation with scale analysis suggests the magnitude of our problems and the need for behavioral theories and methods that derive from specific historical contexts. No doubt, we must continue to borrow from studies of modern institutions. But, in choosing which theories to superimpose on the past, we ought to follow two general principles. First, the assumptions we make ought to be intuitively palatable. Perhaps voting behavior in the nineteenth century was so ideological or party-based as to produce attitudinal stability. Or perhaps what happened on the floor of Congress did not matter, as decisions then, as now, were made elsewhere, in party caucuses, committee rooms, the White House, or the federal bureaucracy. What we know about antebellum Congresses suggests otherwise—that speeches did change votes, that roll calls decided issues, and, given the rapid turnover of members and the embryonic nature of the committee system, that decisions were made at the last minute amid the confusion and clutter of the old Senate and House chambers. While Roy Nichols (1948) and C. Vann Woodward (1956) tell a story using the perspective of the detective, each succeeds in detailing the context in which congressional activity took place. To ignore these portraits of historical behavior is to deny ourselves that cultural intuition which lies at the heart of all behavioral theory. Thus Silbey and Alexander might well have asked themselves, "Do Nichol's congressmen exist in a world of sufficient stability to allow for the development of consistent voting attitudes? And did the Congress of the 1840s, again as sketched by Nichols, use the roll call in such a way as to make scale analysis a reasonable procedure for processing roll call votes?"

Second, we should limit our borrowing to models encouraging maximum adaptation. Scale analysis is simply too powerful a tool for our purposes. Given its theoretical assumptions, the requisite statistical processing is essentially automatic. But its very power compels us to cast our data in a single, narrow form. A less-powerful theory would allow us to better confront our epistemological problems.

The recent work of Donald Matthews and James Stimson (1970) suggests one possibility. Having interviewed hundreds of congressmen, Matthews and Stimson discovered that most vote with little knowledge of the specific issue in question. Caught up in the work of their own committees, they were left with little time to study every or even most bills on which they voted. Instead, most congressmen developed a set of cue givers, men whose opinions and expertise they trusted and whose votes they were willing to imitate. While every congressman developed a unique pattern of cue givers, Matthews and Stimson also discovered certain general features of a system in which party leaders, committee chairmen and ranking members, as well as the leaders of state and regional delegations, become prime candidates for the role of cue givers.

While Matthews and Stimson's interview data are probably rich enough to establish the broad outlines of their general model of congressional voting, they also sought to translate their model into a statistical routine—in part to give in greater detail particular cue patterns, and in part to explain the voting behavior of congressmen we cannot interview. In brief, their technique involves identifying a group of most likely cue givers, and then using agreement scores between cue takers and cue givers on an initial set of roll calls to predict how the cue takers will vote (or rather, did vote) on the next set of roll calls.

The question then becomes, "Can we use their general model and statistical routine?" We can, of course, accept both as a single package, much as we accepted Guttman scaling. But to do so would continue that dependence on others which too often has led us astray. Nor need we accept both theory and technique, since in this case they are eminently divisible. Certainly the notion that congressmen take cues in deciding how to vote is intuitively acceptable in a historical context. We might even accept the general form of Matthews and Stimson's computer model for inferring how, when, and by whom cues are given. But provided we can develop sufficient expertise of our own, there is no reason for us not to build our own statistical models—models which derive directly from the historical context under consideration. I do not want to suggest the cue model is a magical solution. Far from it, for the task of building a working statistical model is enormous, and we must still accept on faith that cue-giving in fact describes how legislators in the past determined how they would vote. But the cue-giving model is worth our attention precisely because its applicability in a historical context depends on our own methodological inventiveness—which, in not too subtle fashion, is the point this essay is trying to make.

Ironically, perhaps, our dependence on our colleagues in political science may no longer be possible, largely because they are in the process of reordering their own priorities. Gone is that sense of euphoria which characterized social research in the 1960s. Gone too is that sense of evangelical mission which portrayed the 1960s as a prelude to a generation of progress in which systematic analysis would establish the parameters of political change. Basic questions once thought answered are being reasked. The efficacy of mathematical modeling is again in doubt, reflecting a general concern that the behavioral sciences, in pursuing technique, have ignored substance. Legislative studies have been particularly affected. The American Political Science Association's Study of Congress Project, after an initial burst of energy, is now moribund. Roll call studies have fallen in favor, and probably the most promising of them—Warren Miller and Donald Stokes' (1963) study comparing the attitudes of congressmen and their constituents—has never been completed. Robert Peabody (1969) suggested that research on Congress had reached

> an important middle stage in its development. Over the last two decades and especially since 1960 a proliferation of empirical studies have yielded much new data, richer insights, and a better understanding of the internal workings of Congress, executive-legislative relationships, and the representative process.

Despite this almost ritualistic recital of past accomplishments, Peabody lamented that "political scientists have not yet produced a conceptually clear and comprehensive theory of congressional behavior."

For most political scientists, however, it was no longer an important issue. A theory of congressional behavior would at best be descriptive. Attempts to build a general theory of legislative behavior had similarly failed, the victims of the uniqueness of any particular legislative setting. Cross-national studies, while interesting, told us more about differences among national political settings than similarities among legislative arenas. What little money remained available for political research was spent elsewhere. The net result is a field now unsure of itself and hence less likely to provide the new ideas and more sophisticated techniques on which historians have come to depend.

Fortunately, we can afford a rather iconoclastic, if not cavalier, attitude toward this lessening of interest in general legislative theory. We will, at long last, be forced to become our own methodologists. Just as importantly, we may also begin using legislative data for more than just political studies, may in fact begin to understand that legislatures within the American context at least, are representative institutions in more than the strictly political and constitutional sense.

Two recent studies provide something of a model for a more broadly based history of legislative behavior. The first is Young (1966), a study of the growth of Washington, D.C., as a political community and the travails of establishing a federal governmental system in the first quarter of the nineteenth century. Though trained as a political scientist, and blessed with the historian's innate sense of time and place, Young in fact adopts the guise of a cultural anthropologist, and his study is an example of a historical ethnography. His concern is not with the political system per se but with the community of men and women who through misfortune and avarice as well as personal ambition found themselves living in a swamp, unwanted, often unwashed, and frequently disparaging their own right to govern. They were a government "at a distance and out of sight," having been conveniently forgotten by the citizenry who had dispatched them to do the new nation's bidding.

Washington survived, Young suggests, because the members of this community, particularly those vested with official responsibilities, did what all American pilgrims had done; they built themselves a city upon a hill. From this initial conception, Young's study flows. Voting patterns were as much a product of social and residential groups as of sectional interest and jealousies. Leadership came to those who helped knit the community together, while the transient nature of Washington life guaranteed a sense of impermanence which made social amelioration all the more crucial, even at the cost of effective political leadership. The presidency as the one stable, seemingly permanent fixture came to dominate Congress, in no small part because the congressmen themselves were absorbed with the constant task of community-building.

The survival of Washington both as political community and seat of government, and the pattern of constitutional prerogatives and responsibilities which emerged from this struggle provide the central focus of Young's study. Taking advantage of the richness of his political data, he dealt essentially with the problem of community-building in nineteenth-century America. All the ingredients were there—the naive faith that communities could be planned and nature overcome, the curious mixture of idealism and avarice which fueled more than one land boom, the importance of personal accommodation, and, above all, that sense of community with its emphasis on conformity in the face of social flux which characterized so much of America's early development. The second study, by Nelson Polsby (1968), makes the same point in a quite different context. Polsby's interest in legislative history stemmed from both a general concern with the institutionalization of social organizations and a more particular interest in the process by which a highly specialized political institution can remain representative. The modern U.S. House of Representatives, Polsby argued, was precisely such an organization. Its reliance on seniority (and concomitant emphasis on an apprenticeship for new members) is a prime example of the kind of axiomatic procedures we now believe are characteristic of highly institutionalized organizations. The codification and division of House business in terms of standing committees reflects the inherent complexity of the modern legislative process. The emphasis on a professional ethic among career congressmen testifies to the institution's boundedness and separation from the ways of the larger society. Put another way, the modern Congress, as even the most casual visitor quickly learns, is a world unto itself, complex, strange, possessed of its own values and rules, and seemingly impervious to the eddies of discontent which frequently swirl about it.

Most congressional research builds on this commonly accepted portrait, describing the internal workings of a committee or the specific advantages of seniority or the particular requirements of a given legislative role. For Polsby, these were no longer interesting questions. We know what Congress is like, what we do not know is how it came to be that way. At what point did Congress separate itself from the rest of society? When did the professional legislator become preeminent? In short, how, when, and why did the House undergo the process of institutionalization?

The bulk of Polsby's brief article is devoted to developing a series of initial measures of institutionalization—measures which focus primarily on the development of a stable membership, the growth of standing committees, the emergence of seniority, and the evolution of a set of uniquely congressional rules of decorum. Polsby, like historians of the late nineteenth century, labeled the period just after 1890 as something of a watershed —or, as Polsby, using the metaphors of economic growth, suggests:

> Some of our indicators give conditional support for a "take-off" theory of modernization. If one of the stigmata of the take-off to modernity is the rapid development of universalistic, bounded, complex institutional forms, the data presented [in this study] . . . lend this theory some plausibility. The "big bang" seems to come in the 1890-1910 period, on at least some of the measures.

Polsby's study is one of those rare breakthroughs which, in summarizing the obvious, recasts our vision. His suggestion that 1890 was a crucial turning point in congressional development not only lends weight to a general belief that American society as a whole was being transformed on the eve of the twentieth century, but, more importantly, his study provides a model for describing how businesses, churches, fraternal organizations, labor unions, local political units, and so on have become institutionalized. Nor is it simply coincidental that Polsby's achievement employed legislative data. His study required a rich theoretical literature, on the one hand, and an equally rich data base on the other—a data base which was relatively constant over time so that measures derived for one decade could be used for succeeding decades. And that is precisely what legislative history supplies. We are a people of the law, fascinated by both its creation and its enforcement. No other American activity, save perhaps the workings of the presidency, has been so faithfully preserved. In most research libraries, for example, the *Congressional Record* (and its antecedents) along with the published volumes of congressional documents take up row upon row of shelving. No archive is complete without at least one and probably a dozen collections of congressional correspondence. We not only know the names of every congressman, but how he (and occasionally she) voted on literally hundreds of issues. We know what they said, where they lived, what they did before and after election to Congress. And what is true of Congress is almost as true of state legislatures. We are truly awash in a sea of legislative data.

This, of course, is hardly a novel observation. The question has always been, "What shall we do with such riches?" One possibility is to continue much as before, using legislative data both to describe the legislative process and to depict major political crises. To do so, however, would mean accepting the dictum that political data can only answer political questions and that a better understanding of legislative behavior can tell us little about the larger society whose interests legislatures claim to represent. There is an alternative, as Polsby suggests. Clearly, once the process of institutionalization is complete, legislatures replete with their own value systems and ways of doing things no longer can be said to reflect (though may continue to represent) the interests of the larger community. Conversely, whenever we study legislatures which have yet to become institutionalized, we essentially study social organizations which are not well bounded and have not created complex internal mechanisms capable of routinizing the way in which decisions are made. Again following Polsby, such institutions would be characterized by a rapid turnover in membership, by the relative unimportance of seniority or the need to serve an apprenticeship, and finally by the absence of a professionalized legislative ethic capable of defining roles and imposing standards of legislative decorum.

Such legislatures have in fact existed, and they have successfully discharged their legislative functions precisely because their values, work habits, and deference patterns were supplied by the larger society. The Massachusetts Assembly in the eighteenth century is one example. Despite the absence of standing committees, seniority, stable membership, and a codified legislative process, the Massachusetts Assembly regularly enacted laws, imposed taxes, and distributed patronage —the chief functions of an eighteenth-century legislature.

Seniority was unimportant because the assembly drew its leaders from among the ranks of the colony's social notables and professional politicians, men who, on the basis of their standing in the community at large, were entitled to power and influence. Legislative practices were similarly borrowed. For most of the eighteenth century, the assembly met in the old Town House, an imposing two-story structure whose ground floor housed Boston's merchant exchange. In many ways, what happened upstairs was indistinguishable from what happened below. Men met, talked, and formed small groups to further some mutual enterprise. In the exchange, these groups were temporary partnerships; in the assembly they were ad hoc committees. The rules of decorum were the same for everybody—men were expected to keep their word, to be forthright, and, in moments of crisis, to be men of principle (Zemsky, 1971).

What I am suggesting is that a noninstitutionalized legislature is a very special microcosm of the society it serves. Given the richness of legislative data and, hence, our ability to describe behavior in remarkably precise terms, we can measure many of the social forces at work within the larger society. How was power and influence distributed? How did men deal with one another? What role did ideologies or belief systems play in organizating private as well as public issues? Colonial historians, for example, have long argued over the role deference and social status played in the eighteenth century. The data supplied by the Massachusetts Assembly affords a remarkable opportunity to build a model capable of identifying that small group of notables who had inherited social prestige and, hence, political power. Other legislatures offer similar opportunities. If the South was indeed a unique region, its legislatures ought to have reflected those differerences. Frontier legislatures offer a unique opportunity to study the process of community-building. And, as Polsby suggests, the process of institutionalization itself —when and under what conditions it was encouraged or retarded—can become an index of the ebb and flow of institutional forces in American life.

As models, Polsby and Young's studies raise a question of form and function. From beginning to end, Polsby's is an exercise in theory and measurement. He commences with a pair of general propositions about how complex political institutions ensure stability as well as remain representative. Next is sketched, in axiom form, a basic theory of institutionalization from which flows a series of quantifiable measures. Supplementing the statistical time series are a set of congressional attitudes combed from a rich treasure of congressional anecdotes—good stories suggesting the limits of acceptable behavior at particular points in time. From this melange of measured data, Polsby extracts two new propositions. The first is descriptive, outlining the pace of institutionalization which culminated with the "big bang" sometime between 1890 and 1910. The other, a product of theoretical serendipity, becomes a general comment on the process of institutionalization.

> The study of the institutionalization of the House affords us a perspective from which to comment upon the process in general. First, as to its reversibility. Many of our indicators show a substantial decay in the instititional structure of the House in the period surrounding the Civil War. . . . As institutions grow, our expectations about the displacement of resources inward do give us warrant to predict that they will resist decay, but the indications of curvelinearity in our present findings give . . . ample warning that institutions are also continuously subject to environmental influence and their power to modify and channel that influence is bound to be less than all encompassing.

Here Polsby becomes the quintessential historian concerned with time, place, and circumstance. He is interested in the past precisely because it is unique and, hence, can expand the known range of human behavior. He begins—as I think most historians in fact begin—with an image of the present and then asks how different the past was from the present? While his reliance on theory both to structure his understanding of the present and to suggest measures of difference makes his comparisons more explicit, at heart his study rests on a basic intuition about human behavior, institutions in general, and congressional behavior in particular. True, Polsby has eschewed plot and was not very interested in people ,or issues. Instead, he explored what he considered the natural history of an institution.

Though Young's study encompassed a smaller chunk of time, it also builds on an informed presentmindedness, one that explains a past society by relying on a theoretical framework for depicting political relationships. Young, however, makes theory subsidiary to description. In the best sense, he tells a story, focusing on individuals, issues, and the vicissitudes of circumstance. He wants to know what happened and why. But in seeking these answers, he returns invariably to basic theory, for in the unraveling of the how and why he seeks, like Polsby, to define the parameters of political change.

By custom, review essays are expected to be prescriptive as well as descriptive. I am leery of suggesting a single model for future studies of legislative behavior; instead, I offer three general observations of where we might go from here.

First, we must become our own theorists (and, by extension, our own methodologists). We should do so, in part because no one else is interested in our problems, but mostly because the past, as Polsby and Young demonstrate can in fact broaden and not infrequently correct our general understanding of how political and other institutions change over time.

Second, we should make our peace with traditional, narrative-based history. There is no objective truth, and no matter how sophisticated our statistical models become, they cannot exist detached from the particular context we study. All endeavor is based on intuition, and traditional studies, such as Nichols (1948) and Woodward (1956), can supply a much-needed sense of context for our more abstract endeavors.

Third, we should be more exploitive of our legislative data, being concerned with processes as well as events and explicitly studying legislatures because often they reflect social forces at work within the larger society. Traditionally, the historian has claimed the role of generalist and synthesizer. It is a role we should not abandon simply because the behavioral sciences have carved up human experience into a set of mutually exclusive categories. If we are to again become generalists, we must reestablish our independence, by building our own models, developing our own methods, and constructing our own theories.

REFERENCES

ALEXANDER, T. B. (1967) Sectional Stress and Party Strength: A Study of Roll Call Voting Patterns in the United States House of Representatives 1836-1860. Nashville: Vanderbilt Univ. Press.

MATTHEWS, D. and J. STIMSON (1970) "Decision making by U.S. representatives," in S. Ulmer (ed.) Political Decision Making. New York: D. Van Nostrand.

MILLER, W. and D. STOKES (1963) "Constituency influence in Congress." Amer. Pol. Sci. Rev. 57: 45-57.

NICHOLS, R. (1948) The Disruption of American Democracy. New York: Macmillan.

PEABODY, R. (1969) "Research on Congress," in D. Huitt and R. Peabody, Congress: Two Decades of Analysis. New York: Harper & Row.

POLSBY, N. (1968) "The institutionalization of the U.S. House of Representatives." Amer. Pol. Sci. Rev. 62: 144-68.

PRICE, A. D. (1963) "Are Southern Democrats different?" in N. Polsby et al., Politics and Social Life. Boston: Houghton Mifflin.

SILBEY, J. (1967) The Shrine of Party: Congressional Voting Behavior 1841-1852. Pittsburgh: Univ. of Pittsburgh Press.

WOODWARD, C. V. (1965) Article in New York Times (January 24); sect. 7, 44.

——— (1956) Reunion and Reaction. Garden City, N.Y.: Doubleday.

YOUNG, J. S. (1966) The Washington Community. New York: Columbia Univ. Press.

ZEMSKY, R. (1971) Merchants, Farmers and River Gods. Boston: Gambit.

Stratification and Community Political Systems

Historians' Models

ROBERT R. DYKSTRA
University of Iowa

Although there are other definitions of the term, to many sophisticated scholars theoretical models come in two forms: (1) testable representations of existing theory, and (2) initial abstractions out of which theory is hopefully expected to develop (Harvey, 1969: 144-151). American social historians have long presumed a functional relationship between a community's stratification system and its political system. But precious little has emerged in historical literature that would qualify as models of this relationship. For one thing, the disinclination of historical research to profess any theoretical positions whatsoever is proverbial. For another, few historians have been courageous enough to offer generalizations invested with very wide-ranging applicability. We have normally been content with posing relatively modest suggestions about the "general significance" of our research, an intradisciplinary timidity I confess to having shared. The time is ripe for a preliminary assessment of the little that *has* been provided in this line.

Let us at the outset dispose of a conventional preconception. The formulations of neither Karl Marx nor Max Weber, while more than relevant to any theoretical contemplation of the subject addressed here, has yet been cast in forms adequate to practical testability. These two great pioneer social analysts are often viewed as offering alternative universal models (Janowitz, 1970: 7-9).[1] Accordingly, to Marx the particular social structure generated by the prevailing mode of production in a given society is the independent variable that produces the society's political system. Hence understanding its class configuration is equivalent to comprehending its politics. In alleged contrast, Weber sees the relationship as much more complex, holding that class, social status, and political power are discrete variables, each with its own hierarchy structure, each possessing its own dynamics of change. A community's political system is thus derived from the particular manner in which these three variables converge, conflict, and otherwise interact.

But it seems to me that any such simplification is oversimplification. There is, for instance, far more latitude for rich conceptual variety within contemporary Marxist scholarship than the mechanistic class-struggle scenario frequently attributed to it.[2] True enough, by sheer definition, those who own the means of production constitute the ruling class. But, within the dominant stratum, conflicts may be expected between landed gentry and capitalists, and even among capitalists themselves as new forms of technology assert their feasibility. The only cohesiveness within the ruling class absolutely insisted upon by a Marxian approach is that, as a class, it will consistently labor to maintain its dominant position. Moreover, with respect to the subordinate strata "class consciousness" is a prescriptive rather than descriptive characteristic, so that, in terms of the United States especially, the influence of ethnicity, race, and religion are hardly to be discounted.[3] In many respects, then, a sophisticated Marxian treatment in a given instance may outwardly exhibit the pluralism normally associated with a Weberian analysis.

Neither is Weber sufficiently explicit to be considered as providing a very practical alternative to Marx. For example, his distinction between class and status would seem so subtle as to defy empirical application. "Property [or wealth] as such," remarks Weber, "is not always recognized as a status qualification, but in the long run it is, and with extraordinary regularity." But furthermore,

> social honor [that is, status] can stick directly to a class-situation, and it is also, indeed most of the time, determined by the average class-situation of the status-group members. This, however, is not necessarily the case. Status membership, in turn, influences the class-situation in that the style of life required by status groups makes them prefer special kinds of property or gainful pursuits and reject others [Weber in Gerth and Mills, 1946: 187, 405].

The lack of some clear notion of at least *when* such convergences may be expected to occur points to a representative difficulty.[4]

To more perceptive minds than mine, of course, models may lurk in the Germanic prose of Marx and Weber. And if one accepts the dictum that "men think in terms of models" (Deutsch, 1963: 19), it may indeed be that empirical studies of stratification and community politics implicitly conform in some essential manner to either universal formulation. It is my view, however, that attempting to wrestle a given piece of analysis into any dichotomous Marxian/Weberian classification scheme is likely to be an exercise in ultimate frustration. The most, I think, that can be said in this vein is that, in practice, a Weberian analysis is more likely to treat politics as meriting singular inquiry as an independent source of social change (Janowitz, 1970: 8), while a Marxian treatment may tend to lavish so much attention on stratification as to allow politics to seem almost irrelevant.[5] In addition, a Weberian treatment may appear more philosophically tolerant of, say, a distribution of community political power that seems unrelated in any causal sense with the community's distribution of wealth or social status (for example, see Lemon and Nash, 1968).

But even these distinctions are suggested only tentatively, since they probably would not hold up in many examples of empirical writings by self-conscious Marxists or Weberians. And they fail to accommodate such occasional problematical cases as that of a New Left-approved study organized around what appears to be a specific Weberian construction (compare Gutman, 1963: 41; O'Brien et al., 1970: 91).

My own survey of the historical literature exploring the relationship of stratification and community political systems has unearthed only two formulations that would appear to merit description as models.

THE ELKINS-McKITRICK MODEL

This represents an authentic model in one of Harvey's senses: a simplified representation of an existing theory. Stanley Elkins and Eric McKitrick (1954) provide a restatement of Frederick Jackson Turner's controversial theory that American political democracy owed its unique qualities to some causal sequence arising from the frontier experience—an impressionistically convincing notion, they observe, that hitherto lacked only an empirical foundation.

Drawing on an unpublished sociological study, the authors (1954: 325) identify political democracy as

a manipulative attitude toward government, . . . a wide participation in public affairs, a diffusion of leadership, a widespread sense of personal competence to make a difference [that] evolves most quickly during the initial stages of setting up a new community; it is seen most dramatically while the process of organization and the solving of basic problems are still crucial; it is observed to best advantage when this flow of basic problems is met by a homogeneous population.

"Homogeneity" means "a similar level of social and economic status and aspirations among the people," and also the absence of "a traditional, ready-made structure of leadership in the community"—that is, political homogeneity as well.

The authors then project this cluster of definitions against the local political systems of three regional frontiers: the

Massachusetts Bay Colony, the ante bellum South, and the Old Northwest. The Massachusetts experience, to the authors, admirably illustrates the Turnerian response to problems inherent in organizing new communities by a relatively homogeneous population bent on individual economic success. Though the colony's charter made no provision for local government, its founders had in mind closely knit settlements on the lines of the English village. Out of this desire evolved the town as a local residential format, the legal status and administrative details of which remained to be innovated. Necessity proved the mother of invention on the New England frontier (Elkins and McKitrick, 1954: 589):

> The town's isolation and lack of prior institutions, combined with the high aspirations of the people, immediately produced the widest range of problems to be dealt with; standards were to be maintained under conditions demanding a level of combined effort for which the settlers' prior experience had little prepared them.

Schools had to be organized, meeting houses built, fences and roads constructed and maintained. Soon these settlers saw the need for some mechanism by which all local talents could be brought together for a collective approach to common problems. They therefore invented the town meeting. In 1635/6, the Massachusetts General Court acknowledged the right of local people to handle their own affairs (1954: 590-591).

> This "right," together with a broad and energetic participation in the concerns of the town itself, was more accurately a matter of stark necessity than either a right or a privilege. Moreover, with property ownership almost universal and with the need for all available talent crucial and pressing, the niceties of the [original] church-membership qualification for citizenship [or "freemanship"] could scarcely afford to be read too literally.

In 1647, therefore, the General Court allowed nonfreemen to serve on boards of selectmen, and set up provisions for fining church members who deliberately avoided presenting themselves for freemanship to escape public service. Thus had New England's democratic system emerged at the local level. The frontier of the ante bellum South provided the exception that proves the rule. Focusing attention on pioneer Alabama and Mississippi, Elkins and McKitrick see two factors frustrating the emergence of local democracy. The first was an incoming planter class that rapidly monopolized economic opportunity, social status, and political power. The second factor was an economy dominated by cotton monoculture. Out of this came a community of little internal diversity, with the plantation as the center of all social and economic life. Hence, no multiplicity of local problems emerged. Those that did were easily handled by the planter elite to whose leadership common folk deferred. Local government in ante bellum Mississippi and Alabama remained simple in character and rather exclusively functional at the county level, a political circumstance generally true for the entire cotton-growing South.

The prime instrument of local administration was the county court system that had originated in the older seaboard colonies (1954: 573). "Functionally the system [had] met for generations all the tests of structured leadership: acceptance, respect, and transmissibility of power." With few changes, the system was carried into the nineteenth century: "its simple structure was not experimented with by subdividing its powers among townships and school districts, and there were few towns to provide independent nuclei of political activity and power" (1954: 575). Not even "Jacksonian Democracy" was later able to modify these authoritarian local political systems, being confined to the expression of an egalitarian rhetorical style that never objectively threatened the status quo.

In the authors' view, democracy evolved *most* fully where the early population was most homogeneous, the small town most prevalent, local governmental forms most pluralistic, and the range of problems greatest: the Old Northwest. Initial community formation in Ohio, Indiana, and Illinois was more than a simple recapitulation of Massachusetts Bay. It was a reenactment rid of all Puritan inhibition, a harmonious festival of collective innovation and individual opportunity. And once the problem-solving era faded, once the community's basic arrangements had been stabilized, a variety of civic needs demanded by a burgeoning small-town capitalism kept public life open and dynamic. Not by accident, the authors note, had Turner drawn the major inspiration for his famous theory from the frontier experience of the older Middle West.

The authors' model represents a brilliant employment of secondary materials. How has it fared in light of some important and more recent empirical research?

Elkins and McKitrick (1954: 598 n.) observe that a then recent article by B. Katherine Brown (1954) supported their model by demonstrating that in the Bay Colony restrictions on office-holding and voting by nonfreemen at the local level were of minimal importance, and that qualifications for freemanship were liberal and the numbers of freemen consequently much larger than previously supposed. Soon extended to eighteenth-century Massachusetts by Robert E. Brown (1955), this new view touched off an avalanche of scholarship that ignored the Elkins-McKitrick model while often implicitly commenting on it. The vast bulk of the criticism directed toward the Browns was both negative and narrowly concerned with their sampling techniques and statistical manipulations with respect to the extent of the Massachusetts franchise. And much of it assumed a somewhat irrelevant cast with the introduction (Pole, 1962) of the concept of "deferential" politics, plausibly suggesting that a largely enfranchised Colonial voting population everywhere routinely endorsed the political hegemony of the social and economic elite.

Of course, the role of elites is one of the most difficult factors the model must come to grips with. Elkins and McKitrick (1954: 567) prove a bit elusive here, allowing that "success, prominence and power" are "limited ultimately to a fraction . . . in any society," although what distinguished the South was that "the fraction was smaller, and mobility within it less. . . . Here, *initial* prominence and power counted for more."

The authors' failure to offer some quantitative definition of "small" and "rigid," however, makes application of this insight particularly tricky.

Space limitations preclude anything approaching full bibliographic elaboration of the many case studies that have been drawn from Colonial Massachusetts. But two of them seem especially useful. At first blush, the experience of seventeenth-century Sudbury seems to conform to the Elkins-McKitrick model. As presented by Sumner Chilton Powell (1963), early Sudbury comprised a socially homogeneous population facing the many problems incident to founding a new community. Such problems were all faithfully brought up in monthly town meetings for the surprisingly harmonious collective disposition by "free townsmen" (resident landowners). But also, within a few years, citizens elected their first board of selectmen to provide ongoing executive administration, also investing it with authority to make new land grants. While a small core of the larger landholders repeatedly served as selectmen, the board was not, in Powell's (1963: 129) estimate, an exclusive body: "At least thirty-nine different men, 52 per cent of the male land grantees, served as selectmen during the period 1639-1655." Yet if one closely scrutinizes Powell's data it also becomes abundantly clear that just eight men, or 17% of the total grantees, served as selectmen six or more terms, in fact filling 57% of *all* available local governmental posts during the period. This included a virtual monopoly—fourteen of sixteen terms—of the local judiciary. Moreover, these eight men granted one another fully 36% of the land in Sudbury (all percentages calculated from Powell, 1963: 229-230). To the author (Powell, 1963: 128) it was simply that "the citizens expected that their large landowners would give almost unlimited time and service to affairs of the town." Wealth and social position had their liabilities, presumably.

Kenneth A. Lockridge (1970) takes a less charitable view of a similar situation in Dedham. Between 1639 and 1687 just ten Dedham men, perhaps 5% of the adult male residents, filled 60% of the selectmen's terms. All ten were also in the top third taxpaying bracket locally, seven in the upper sixth, and five in the top tenth. "Wealth," notes Lockridge (1970: 43), "was not everything—some men from the lower ranks were called to office—but it helped." Until late in the century, the vaunted town meeting at Dedham provided hardly more than a periodic ratification of the elite's decisions, a phenomenon Lockridge aptly labels "conservative corporate voluntarism" and feels arose out of a dread of social conflict combined with an ideology of Christian solidarity that imposed restraints on both leaders and led.

In the larger historiographical context, Lockridge (1970: 194) generalizes from both his own and others' research in concluding that

> a sort of consensus on the substance of early Massachusetts politics is emerging. While both Puritan political theory and English village practices put a high value on popular participation, both in theory and in practice there were strong countervailing emphases on peace, order, and consensual unity which were antithetical to "democracy" in today's sense of a society of equal individuals possessing both the freedom and the power to dissent.

A gradual constriction of the originally wide local suffrage occurred in Massachusetts, until by the late 1680s perhaps most adult males held no franchise whatever. But this is only one part of the story; deferential politics was the other (Lockridge, 1970: 194):

> Even in the period of high suffrage, townsmen had used their votes to elect repeatedly a few, relatively wealthy leaders. They had rarely questioned the decisions of that leadership. So, all in all, while hardly an out-and-out oligarchy, this system was no "democracy" in any sense familiar to Americans today. Only with a string of qualifying adjectives can that word be applied to early Massachusetts.

Meanwhile, the Elkins-McKitrick model as it pertains to the ante bellum South has gone virtually unnoticed.[6] With respect to the Old Northwest it received its most explicit attention—if repeated and wholly uncritical anthologization merits this phrase. Only Allan G. Bogue (1960: 27-28) early broke ranks by citing certain methodological deficiencies in the model, also identifying difficulties in making it conform to Midwestern frontier realities, especially with respect to socioeconomic homogeneity. The monumental application of Turnerian theory by Merle Curti (1959) also ignored the Elkins-McKitrick model; at the same time one of the model's authors (McKitrick, 1959: 20) certified that early Midwestern democracy stood in no great need of elaborate substantiation:

> He [Curti] knew before he began that it was precisely on the frontier that he would find democracy in all its churning and bubbling vitality. The problem was not really "proving" that democracy existed here—certainly there should be things in this culture that do not require "proof" in the narrow sense—but rather of demonstrating it in its various workings, of showing how the thing was acted out.

Nevertheless, the skeptical mentality finds Curti's treatment of elite behavior amid all this social effervescence of something more than marginal interest.

Trempealeau County, Wisconsin, established in 1854, remained heavily rural through the period of the study. Property holding proved expectedly widespread, but unexpectedly top heavy in terms of distribution, a mere 10% of landowners commanding 39% of the real property valuations in both 1860 and 1870. (This was, significantly, a configuration identical to that found in a control group of Vermont townships sampled for the same years.) Though probably most males were eligible voters, and there was a "reasonable fluidity" of turnover among local men from the higher propertied ranks, this tendency accelerated as the county gradually shed its frontier character.

In a somewhat larger context, in which office-holding and property were themselves employed among a number of variables, Curti discusses 155 men he considers to have been the county's most important political leaders. Although the large majority were farmers, for the post-1860 era business and professional men were clearly overrepresented in this elite in comparison to their percentages among the county's gainfully employed. This fact Curti (1959: 440) oddly discounts, perhaps to buttress his subsequent assertion that "our studies have not given support to [what is perhaps the Elkins-McKitrick] hypothesis that leadership in a growing community is likely to come from the towns."

Even more pertinent is his finding (1959: 426) that "it is in amount of property that leaders differ most from the gainfully employed in general. . . . In the later [post-1860] period the difference seems somewhat sharper, suggesting that money may not have been so important a factor in successful leadership in the definitely frontier period." The initial conclusion is consistent with Curti's data; the qualifier is hardly that, being based on the difference between a percentage-point overrepresentation by the $1,000-plus bracket of 23 in 1860 and 32 in 1870 (calculated from Curti, 1959: 420). Even in the county's "frontier" era property was not everything in determining leadership status—but it helped. Thereafter it helped even more.

The refrain of the author's (1959: 378) treatment of Trempealeau's political system was that it was democratic: "the rank and file . . . felt that the decisions made on the major issues did reflect, reasonably well, the search for majority interest and majority preference." His single reservation is with respect to the widespread use of the political caucus, a device that "enabled a few men, in the decision-making process, to give undue weight to their own ambitions, personal grudges, and interpretations of parochial interests." Yet only in passing does he note the existence of a "cohesive and enduring" clique composed of seven commercial farmers, lawyers, and businessmen whom he elsewhere includes among the county's wealthiest and most persistent office-holders. One of the seven was the single most politically powerful man in the county. Curti's failure to provide specifics about the functions of this special elite seems a strange and slightly ominous omission in a "case study of democracy" that spans nearly five hundred printed pages. But we must leave it at that.

Recently my own research in the social history of the Kansas cattle-trading centers of the 1870s and 1880s (Dykstra, 1968) led me to question an especially fundamental proposition of the Elkins-McKitrick model: that local democracy in a frontier setting is to be conceived of as a kind of corporate routine in which community "problems" provoked collective responses and in which local politics was largely a talent hunt for the best men to fill administrative jobs at hand. Here the main insight offered is that "local democracy" could take two forms: (1) the "ordinary democratic process" in which decision-making was managed by an elite that was in turn regularly ratified by an electorate, and (2) community conflict, wherein problems were really *issues* that stimulated a polarity of positions and consequently mobilized an electorate to political warfare. The first seems to be what Lockridge means by "conservative corporate voluntarism." It prevailed at Dedham except for a somewhat mysterious episode of 1660 wherein citizens over-turned the entire board of selectmen; it prevailed at Sudbury except in 1655/6 when the issue of land distribution split voters into factions, with a similar result. It was apparently present in Trempealeau County except when prohibition and the county-seat location question sometimes became issues. In these cases conflict briefly became the decision-making mode.

At the Kansas cattle towns, I discovered both forms operating in both town and county politics, although clearly the "ordinary democratic process" allowed the most latitude for elite chicanery. The town of Caldwell provided the most disreputable instance. Here in the years 1881-1884 local business and professional men simply caucused and divided all administrative offices among themselves, the electorate then obediently accepting this decision. Normally, however, business community factionalism—especially a tendency to bifurcate into competing entrepreneurial blocs[7]—as well as the "law-and-order" issue (later sharply accelerated by moral-reform extremism) served to confound the impulse toward a thoroughgoing small-capitalist consensus, keeping voters polarized and issue-oriented. Virulent town-country antagonisms, marked by frequent challenges by farmers of "urban" control of the courthouse, provided the same service with respect to county politics. While Elkins and McKitrick (1954: 340) go so far as to remark on "the ease with which the basic agrarian experience flowed into that of commercial small-urban enterprise," at the cattle towns the rural mood is more plausibly described as an incipient class-consciousness that would later reveal itself in some aspects of Populism.[8]

The foregoing remarks by no means exhaust the possibilities for critical comment on the Elkins-McKitrick model.[9] But let us turn to a second important formulation.

THE PERIPHERY-VERSUS-THE-CENTER MODEL[10]

Also encompassing the problematical relationship between stratification and community politics, this model was introduced by Richard C. Wade (1968) as a means of comprehending the general spatial configuration of urban reform politics in the Progressive Era. It can be considered an abstraction preliminary to some comprehensive theory.

Wade reviews the manner in which the populations of larger American cities in the late nineteenth and early twentieth centuries distributed themselves in response to the urban "mass transit" revolution embodied successively by the omnibus, the horse-drawn railway, the cable car, the street railway, the elevated, the subway, the motor bus, and, ultimately, the automobile. This, says Wade (1968: 194), provided the American metropolis with its "characteristic social profile":

> The outer edges of the city were occupied by the older inhabitants, usually wealthier than others. These pleasant neighborhoods tended to be Protestant in religion and northern European in extraction. At the center were the newcomers, fresh from foreign lands, Catholic and Jewish, lower class in occupation and income. Between the two were the "zones of emergence," increasingly comprised of second- and third-generation immigrants on their way out of the central city and on their way up socially and economically.

This configuration in turn precipitated a new political expression: the periphery against the center. It was in the core area that the "boss" and the "machine" arose in response to the immediate needs of the ethnically diverse and economically deprived (Wade, 1968: 196).

> The boss helped recent arrivals to find housing, secured them jobs, mediated with public authorities, managed families through bad times, and somehow gave the recent arrivals a sense of belonging to their new land. To be sure, the cost was not small—laws were bent and broken; officials corrupted; funds embezzled; the franchises sullied. Essentially, however, the boss system was simply the political expression of inner city life.

From the urban periphery came the attack on the evils of machine politics that characterized the Progressive Era:

> Political organization in these white-collar residential areas was as much an expression of the neighborhood as the boss system was of the congested center. "Reform associations" grew up to protect and advance the concerns of the middle-class constituents of the outlying wards. Thus the characteristic instrument of reform was "the committee of one hundred," or the "committee of seventy-five," etc. Since the neighborhoods were scattered and the interests diverse, the periphery found the broadly based committee more appropriate than the "boss."

Specific issues aside, the "real cleavage went much deeper. The contest was to determine whether the oldest residents or the newcomers would shape the life of the metropolis. Behind the attack on the boss lay thinly disguised hostility to the hyphenated population of the central city" (Wade, 1968: 198). Metropolitan voting patterns increasingly reflected this conflict of periphery and center: "Reform majorities dwindled, then disappeared, as they crossed over the lines demarcating the oldest parts of town."

The single explicit application of the periphery-versus-the-center model as yet produced is Zane L. Miller's study of reform politics in Cincinnati. It seems noteworthy that Wade himself (in Miller, 1968: 'ix) views this important study as having gone well beyond the conventional views of urban politics with their emphasis on ethnicity, political organization, status and class and [adding] a residential dimension. The notion of the periphery and the center is satisfying because it organizes these other elements without excluding them, thus providing a more persuasive synthesis than other approaches.

So endorsed, Miller proceeds to define three major residential areas of Cincinnati in the decades on either side of 1900: "the Circle," the old urban core; "the Zone," the transitional area; and "the Hilltops," the city's fashionable fringe. Each of these areas expressed a distinct political interest, and the shifting interactions of their respective voters, says Miller, explain local conflicts over periodic reform endeavors by social gospelers, philanthropists, civic boosters, and crusaders for municipal efficiency. Miller's (1968: 241) conclusion that each residential area was itself internally heteregeneous leads him to believe that "residence rather than race, religion, or ethnicity provides the touchstone to the city's social and political experience."

This proposition is of course much more radically geographical than is required by the model to which Miller has keyed his interpretation. It also runs afoul of a recent new emphasis on the primacy of ethnocultural factors in explaining political behavior.[11] Joel A. Tarr (1969: 1380) reflects this new-school orientation in castigating Miller's failure to conceptualize residence as merely "a reflection of ethnic, religious, racial, and class factors rather than as an independent variable." Tarr statistically disputes Miller's specific statements that Cincinnati's Hilltop wards were dominated by native whites of native parentage, a criticism that Miller modestly rebuts by altering the wording of the disputed passages in the subsequent paperback edition of his book.

Insofar as nativity and racial data for Cincinnati's wards given in the 1910 federal census do provide at least a partial measurement of social heterogeneity, Miller might well have refined his argument somewhat by concentrating on the social makeup of the "political populations" (that is, adult males) of his three districts. My own calculations (see Table 1) suggest

TABLE 1

AREA DISTRIBUTION (percentage) OF ADULT MALES IN CINCINNATI BY NATIVITY AND RACE, 1910

	Circle[a]	Zone[b]	Hilltops[c]
Native white:			
Native parentage	33.89	29.16	39.54
Foreign or mixed parentage	29.49	41.52	39.29
Foreign-born white	23.83	25.41	18.39
Negro	12.79	3.91	2.78
Total	100.00	100.00	100.00

SOURCES: Miller (1968: 44); U.S. Bureau of the Census (1913: 426-427).
a. Wards 4-8, 15, 16, 18.
b. Wards 3, 9-11, 14, 17, 19-24.
c. Wards 1, 2 12, 13.

that considerable internal diversity did indeed characterize each voting bloc. The political populations of all three areas were over 50% first- or second-generation immigrants. But contrary to Tarr's expectations—and the model's prescription—there was no considerable graduation from more to less immigrant influence as the focus moves from the Circle out to the Hilltops, the immigrant proportion actually being more pronounced in the intermediate Zone than in either of the polar districts. The only dramatic declension from Circle to Hilltops occurred with respect to the city's black voters.

Yet this does not get at what, for the ethnocultural determinists, is the most fundamental variable: religion. Here Miller's own material seems to contradict his heterogeneity argument. Hilltop wards 12 and 13 were "predominantly Protestant," he notes at one point, elsewhere adding that Catholics "were not numerously represented" in the Hilltops (Miller, 1968: 119, 53). Relative to both Circle and Hilltops, the Zone was "Catholic territory" (1968: 37). That the Circle was similarly heavily non-Protestant (except for blacks) is suggested both by Miller's narrative and the 1910 census, the largest contingent of foreign-born in three of that district's eight wards being Russian in origin, with the Irish-born sharing this distinction with the German-born in three of its other wards.[12]

Still, Miller is *not* viewing residence as an absolutely independent variable, since wealth was a significant determinant of spatial aggregation. In the Circle, he says, "Poverty was the common denominator"; the Zone was "middle class" in many respects, containing both workers and some of "the city's new rich"; the Hilltops constituted the "high-income districts" from which even skilled workers were excluded (Miller, 1968: 15, 33, 47). (When the author speaks of the Hilltops as being "occupationally" diverse, he is simply referring to a variety of upper-income occupations.) In that the ratio of families to houses is often considered a crude index of relative poverty, my calculations from the 1910 census bear out Miller's characterizations. In the Circle, the ratio was 2.33 families to every house; in the Zone it was 1.78; in the Hilltops, 1.34. Under the terms of the author's treatment, therefore, the periphery-versus-the-center model is fundamentally a class-conflict model.

Perhaps Miller's most important—though unspecified—revision of Wade's formulation lies in his perception of the role of Cincinnati's political boss, George B. Cox. Cox and his Republican machine were not "simply the political expression of inner city life." Although a saloon owner whose personal base was the Circle's eighteenth ward, Boss Cox achieved his power by being a mediator between the moral-reform fanaticism largely originating from the Hilltops and the resistance this generated there as elsewhere. The trick was to offer upper-class voters conventional "progressive" reforms (fiscal responsibility, governmental efficiency, and so forth) while making only minimal adjustments with respect to enforcing blue laws and otherwise responding to moralistic demands. Boss Cox was himself, then, a reformer—but what in my own book (Dykstra, 1968) I call a "moderate reformer." The imperatives of the moderate position on reform reflected the values and attitudes of the local business elite: obsessed with the community image, hostile to moral fanaticism, ultimately rationalizing alterations of the status quo in entrepreneurial terms. What A. B. Webster's leadership meant in the 1880s to troubled Dodge City, what Albert Colson was to Caldwell, Boss Cox offered Cincinnati a decade later. In all three cases dynamic leadership emerged as a centrist response to a community polarization on reform.

Which is about as far as I would care to go at present in suggesting my own version of a model. Meanwhile, the periphery-versus-the-center model, like the Elkins-McKitrick model, may seem an imperfect formulation in several respects. But imperfection is the hazard built into any relatively precise statement designed for general application. American social history stands in need of models to organize its untidy plethora of random monographic insights. The hazards should not be allowed to inhibit thoughtful response to that need.

NOTES

1. Marx and Weber are often discussed in this dual manner with respect to various theoretical aspects of social stratification. For other representative usages, see Barber (1967) and Davies (1970: 11-28).

2. For a sophisticated Marxist treatment of the difference between "serious" and "vulgar" Marxian scholarship, see Genovese (1968). Genovese, however, is not without his own critics on the left, some of whom take issue with his scholarly perceptions (Bluestone, 1969). A sympathetic and fairly sophisticated survey of New Left historiography on American topics is offered by O'Brien et al. (1970).

3. Any historian familiar with the empirical literature should be able to recall instances where an Americanist's discovery of racial and ethnocultural factors has been celebrated as an important undermining of Marxian truth. Yet see Marx and Engels (1953: 242, 258) for brief expressions of Engels' special sensitivity to the political and social ramifications of these factors in the United States.

4. Weber's specific comments on the United States, insofar as they are known to American scholars, are interesting but not surpassingly helpful. As many are aware, Weber was particularly impressed by the role of the American party boss, which informed his view of political power as an independent phenomenon (Gerth and Mills, 1946: 107-111, 194-195, 211).

5. This, I think, is a point made by Frisch (1969: 277), although Frisch does not identify the approach as Marxian.

6. The only specific evaluation I have found is by Lynd (1967: 139), who feels that the model helps solve what was for Turner a serious dilemma: the existence of an anti-democratic frontier. In that the Elkins-McKitrick formulation sees the Southern county court system as a Colonial survival, a book arguing the existence of "middle class democracy" in eighteenth-century Virginia (Brown and Brown, 1964) might be considered a pertinent contradiction of the model. But the scholarly judgment of this book has been overwhelmingly negative, and there seems little to be gained from pursuing the issues raised by it.

7. Business-community bifurcation in the small-urban setting of the nineteenth century seems to have gone virtually unnoticed by social and "urban" historians, in part because contemporary materials tend to conceal the evidence (Dykstra, 1968: 361-366, 382-383). Community sociologists occasionally note such phenomena, however. For example, Schulze (1961: 32) displays a table of "business links among associated economic dominants" in the "Cibola City" of 1860-1900 that documents a split, but he offers little explanation of it, being intent on explaining a later bifurcation.

8. This, too, has been universally overlooked as an important parameter of social conflict in nineteenth-century America. Of major state or regional treatments, only Woodward (1951) and Lamar (1956) elevate it into anything like a general theme.

9. For a number of additional specifics, see Dykstra (1968: 371-378).

10. This is the designation suggested by Stave (1972: 75).

11. Several recently published full-length works employ the ethnocultural approach. For the best recent overview, see Swierenga (1971).

12. It might also be noted that in identifying a diversity of religious persuasions among the members of his Cincinnati reform organizations, Miller may not have allowed for the phenomenon of "tokenism," long acknowledged as useful to any political or social endeavor.

REFERENCES

BARBER, B. (1967) "Social stratification," pp. 288-295 in Volume 15 of International Encyclopedia of the Social Sciences. New York: Macmillan and Free Press.

BLUESTONE, D. M. (1969) "Marxism without Marx: the consensus-conflict of Eugene Genovese." Sci. and Society 33 (Spring): 231-243.

BOGUE, A. G. (1960) "Social theory and the pioneer." Agricultural History 34 (January): 21-34.

BROWN, B. K. (1954) "Freemanship in Puritan Massachusetts." Amer. Historical Rev. 59 (July): 865-883.

BROWN, R. E. (1955) Middle-Class Democracy and the Revolution in Massachusetts, 1691-1780. Ithaca: Cornell Univ. Press.

--- and B. K. BROWN (1964) Virginia, 1705-1786: Democracy or Aristocracy? East Lansing: Michigan State Univ. Press.

CURTI, M. (1959) The Making of an American Community: A Case Study of Democracy in a Frontier County. Stanford: Stanford Univ. Press.

DAVIES, I. (1970) Social Mobility and Political Change. New York: Praeger.

DEUTSCH, K. W. (1963) The Nerves of Government: Models of Political Communication and Control. New York: Free Press.

DYKSTRA, R. R. (1968) The Cattle Towns. New York: Alfred A. Knopf.

ELKINS, S. and E. McKITRICK (1954) "A meaning for Turner's frontier." Pol. Sci. Q. 69 (September): 321-353; (December): 565-602.

FRISCH, M. H. (1969) "The community elite and the emergence of urban politics: Springfield, Massachusetts, 1840-1880," pp. 277-296 in S. Thernstrom and R.

Sennett (eds.) Nineteenth-Century Cities: Essays in the New Urban History. New Haven, Conn.: Yale Univ. Press.

GENOVESE, E. D. (1968) "Marxian interpretations of the slave South," pp. 90-125 in B. J. Bernstein (ed.) Towards a New Past: Dissenting Essays in American History. New York: Random House.

GERTH, H. H. and C. W. MILLS (1946) From Max Weber: Essays in Sociology. New York: Oxford Univ. Press.

GUTMAN, H. G. (1963) "The worker's search for power: labor in the Gilded Age," pp. 38-68 in H. W. Morgan (ed.) The Gilded Age. Syracuse: Syracuse Univ. Press.

HARVEY, D. (1969) Explanation in Geography. London: St. Martin's.

JANOWITZ, M. (1970) Political Conflict: Essays in Political Sociology. Chicago: Quadrangle.

LAMAR, H. R. (1956) Dakota Territory, 1861-1889: A Study of Frontier Politics. New Haven, Conn.: Yale Univ. Press.

LEMON, J. T. and G. B. NASH (1968) "The distribution of wealth in eighteenth-century America: a century of change in Chester County, Pennsylvania, 1693-1802." J. of Social History 2 (Fall): 1-24.

LOCKRIDGE, K. A. (1970) A New England Town: The First Hundred Years. New York: W. W. Norton.

LYND, S. (1967) Class Conflict, Slavery, and the United States Constitution. Indianapolis: Bobbs-Merrill.

MARX, K. and F. ENGELS (1953) Letters to Americans, 1848-1895. New York: International.

McKITRICK, E. (1959) "History and statistics." New Leader 42 (June 15): 19-20.

MILLER, Z. L. (1968) Boss Cox's Cincinnati: Urban Politics in the Progressive Era. New York: Oxford Univ. Press.

O'BRIEN, J., A. GORDON, P. BUHLE, J. MARKOWITZ, and R. KEERAN (1970) "'New Left historians' of the 1960s." Radical America 4 (November): 81-106.

POLE, J. R. (1962) "Historians and the problem of early American democracy." Amer. Historical Rev. 67 (April): 626-646.

POWELL, S. C. (1963) Puritan Village: The Formation of a New England Town. Middletown, Conn.: Wesleyan Univ. Press.

SCHULZE, R. O. (1961) "The bifurcation of power in a satellite city," pp. 19-80 in M. Janowitz (ed.) Community Political Systems. New York: Free Press.

STAVE, B. M. [ed.] (1972) Urban Bosses, Machines, and Progressive Reformers. Lexington, Mass.: D. C. Heath.

SWIERENGA, R. P. (1971) "Ethnocultural political analysis: a new approach to American ethnic studies." J. of Amer. Studies 5 (April): 59-79.

TARR, J. A. (1969) Book review in Amer. Historical Rev. 74 (April): 1380-1381.

U.S. Bureau of the Census (1913) Thirteenth Census of the United States, taken in the Year 1910, Volume 3. Washington, D. C.: Government Printing Office.

WADE, R. C. (1968) "Urbanization," pp. 187-205 in C. V. Woodward (ed.) The Comparative Approach to American History. New York: Basic Books.

WOODWARD, C. V. (1951) The Origins of the New South, 1877-1913. Baton Rouge: Louisiana State Univ. Press.

Perspectives on Industrializing Societies

J. ROGERS HOLLINGSWORTH
University of Wisconsin (Madison)

The scholarly approach to the study of history runs somewhat contrary to the needs generated by our society's intellectual perspective. While our society's intellectual horizon has been expanding in both space and time, the study of history has too often remained nationalistic in its concerns and very restricted in terms of concepts, space, and time.

The major problem facing historians may well be the linking of the tendency to specialize on a given geographical area within a relatively narrow time span with a constantly expanding intellectual horizon. To achieve this goal, we must devise strategies which will minimize our tendency to study national history in isolation from the rest of the world. And to do this, I suggest that we become much more comparative in our approach to the study of history.

If we move toward a more comparative historical analysis, most historians will no doubt continue to study a single society within the relatively narrow confines of space and time—for the historical sources and training required to study more than one society in depth are formidable. Even though we continue to work with a single society, we could nevertheless work with systematically and explicitly stated conceptual frameworks. Working with configurative analysis or with a single case within the context of a comparative historical framework will nevertheless represent an important advance over much of our present research which also tends to focus on single societies. For if we use an explicitly stated conceptual framework or model, we will then be in a position to stimulate numerous case studies of particular kinds of phenomena occurring in many different places and at different points in time. We then enhance the possibilities of abstracting common properties and testing hypotheses. In other words, there is no contradiction between a historical case study approach and the effort to work comparatively.

The comparative analysis may begin by treating a social system as an aggregate of components, all changing, but with varying rates. Analytically, one may define the components and then investigate the way the changes in one component are related to changes in other components, how such components as structures, culture, elites, groups, and policies are linked together. In other words, one may proceed by assessing the changes in the economic structure, by observing how these changes are related to changes in the social structure, the political structure, political culture, and so on, and by analyzing how changes in leadership are related to the scope and direction of changes in the society's basic structures, and how, in turn, policies change.

It is in this direction that I wish to make a small step, to grapple with the following question: are there common processes with which structural and cultural changes have occurred in the economic development of the North Atlantic community? For the most part, I use illustrations from the United States during the past century and seek to illuminate events in the United States by employing a comparative perspective.

The following generalizations emerge from an eclectic body of social science literature, as well as from my own historical investigation. They are presented in very abbreviated form and deserve further augmentation and elaboration. They fit some countries better than others. However, the purpose of this essay is to encourage historical research which will assess their validity in a number of historical settings. Hopefully, this kind of essay, though of a preliminary nature, will facilitate the convergence of research interests of historians and social scientists.

ECONOMIC STRUCTURE

While countries within the North Atlantic community have industrialized from different starting points, their routes to industrialization have differed, and their rates of industrialization have varied, it is, in each society, the economic system which has been most important in bringing about fundamental structural and cultural change.

Societies with relatively low levels of economic development have regions not only with considerable cultural differences but also with considerable variations in their social, economic, and political structures. Because of this variation, there are serious political cleavages on a regional basis. At high levels of economic development, however, per capita income is more evenly distributed among regions, causing cultural and structural distinctions along regional lines to diminish, with the result that regional political cleavages become less pronounced. In other words, there is, in the history of most countries of the North Atlantic community, a process of regional divergence and convergence: regions tending to diverge in their cultural and structural characteristics at low levels of economic development and to converge at higher levels of development, though the process is much more complicated when ethnic and linguistic groups are distributed on a regional basis.

In the process of economic development, growth does not occur at even rates throughout a society. In the strong regions, there is a cumulative growth, with skilled labor and capital moving from the less-developed to the more-prosperous regions, frequently weakening the poor areas. Because the poor region also has higher fertility rates, its per capita income may even decline. Moreover, the poor region generally lacks entrepreneurial talent, has immature capital markets, and possesses a poorly developed transportation system, while the growing region becomes richer in each of these. The economy of the fast-growing region usually benefits by such government policies as tariff, transportation, and banking legislation and substantial investments in human capital—i.e., education and health. In contrast, the retarded region has much lower investments in both education and medical care—with the result that its population has less capacity to recognize and exploit opportunities for development (Hirschman, 1965; Williamson, 1965; Easterlin, 1961).

In its *first* organizational stage, the production units of the growing region resemble the system described by Adam Smith: there is the owner who manages his enterprise and who works alongside his employees. At the *second* stage of organizational development, the marketing area enlarges and the size of firms increases. As the size of firms increases, the owner-manager becomes more concerned with financial affairs and becomes increasingly separated from his employees.

Of course, growth does take place in the poorer regions, as they ultimately attract capital and skilled labor. Prosperous regions invariably spread their wealth to adjoining areas, and, in this respect, firms in the growing region are especially important, raising capital in the cheapest markets and transferring it to less-developed regions where interest rates are high, wage rates low, and, frequently, sources of supply cheaper. In the long run, both large firms and labor unions narrow regional wage differentials in many industries.

Technological changes and product innovation may alter the structure of costs and prices, generating growth in less-developed regions. Slowly, there is a shift in the pattern of regional income inequality, as per capita income on a regional basis begins to converge (Easterlin, 1961; Williamson, 1965).

Governments are also instrumental in the convergence process. Because opportunities in industry and commerce are less attractive in poor regions, many more ambitious men turn to politics. Consequently, they frequently are able to shape government policies to channel resources from the more developed parts of the country to their own region. In this respect, central governments eventually play an important role in developing for poor regions social overhead capital—i.e., transportation, medical and educational facilities, electric power, and so on. With individual income tax and welfare programs, governments transfer wealth from one region to another. Defense spending, especially during wars, is another common aspect of government programs which push income levels toward regional equality (Easterlin, 1961).

The speed with which convergence occurs is influenced by a host of conditions: to mention but a few, whether investment stimulates forward and backward economic linkages, the quality of human capital, the maturity of capital markets, the rigidity of the social system, rate of population growth, in-out migration rates, and the quality of the communication and transportation systems.

As convergence takes place, technology becomes one of the major driving forces in a highly industrial society, making it possible for productivity to rise, for markets to expand, for the size of firms to grow, and for product specialization to increase. These changes in turn transform the culture and structure of almost every sector of the society. For example, changes in transportation and communication allow many types of organizations to increase in size, making internal relationships more impersonal and institutionalized. Norms based on levels of performance, efficiency, and achievement become pervasive not only within business firms, but throughout the society. Because of the need for coordination, information, and rationalization, a highly industrial society becomes increasingly bureaucratized. With increased emphasis on planning and rationalization within firms, the entrepreneur—the innovator, the person who un-settles things—gives way to managerial and other forms of technical expertise. Within business firms, there is an increasing separation between owners and managers with the real corporate power being held by those who manage the bureaucratic hierarchies. At this point, the economy has entered the *third* organizational stage (Averitt, 1968).

The concentration of economic resources continues, shifting to a *fourth* organizational stage. In this stage, the major objective of elite management is no longer profit maximization but the maximization of assets. Fearful that products may become obsolete, firms diversify and expand into other operations as well as other countries. When one country's economy suffers, the firm may prosper elsewhere. Through expansion, merger, and diversification, the size of firms increases, bringing about considerable economic concentration within a relatively few firms. By 1962, for example, the 100 largest corporations operating in the United States owned 46% of all manufacturing assets in the United States, though there were more than 450,000 manufacturing firms in the country. Whereas the American corporation in an earlier day scanned a national horizon seeking factor-price equalization and economic efficiency, a world of rapid communications, jet aircraft, and declining international freight rates permits corporations to search out markets over many continents and to locate productive units where there are favorable wage rates and raw material prices as well as lower transportation, distribution, and servicing costs (Kindleberger, 1969).

The existence of multinational firms in one society sets in motion a process resembling countervailing power: fearful that they will be reduced to secondary status, firms in other societies also expand, merge, and diversify. As a result, multinational firms emerge with operations throughout the world. Though international corporations have existed for several hundred years, it is only at a higher level of economic development and organization that they appear in considerable numbers. It is not only in operations, but in ownership and management that international firms become increasingly multinational. As a result, the industrial core of world production and trade moves toward oligopoly. Meantime, one of the most important consequences of the fourth stage of organization is the movement of knowledge, capital, and technical and managerial labor across national boundaries with increasing efficiency (Kindleberger, 1969).

The emergence of multinational firms has obvious implications for nation-states, for the autonomy of nation-states declines as national economies become integrated into a corporate international structure. For example, the power of nation-states to plan investments and development, to regulate monetary and fiscal affairs, to manage income and wage levels, and to enforce anti-trust legislation efficiently are somewhat limited by the increased power of multinational firms.

As the multinational firm confronts the political system with external strains, a service-oriented economy confronts the political system with enormous strains from within. The service economy is an inevitable outgrowth of a manufacturing economy (Bell, 1972). One consequence of manufacturing is the increased concentration of population in urban areas, which in itself leads to increasing demands for transportation, sanitation, water supply, education, housing, and a multiplicity of other services.

A circular process begins as the proportions of income spent on necessities drops, and there is more spending for durables and luxury items. Educational and medical facilities expand, leading to ever more demands for a better quality of life. This trend may continue until over half the labor force is in services. For example, six out of every ten workers were employed in the service sector of the American economy in 1968, and one in six was a government employee. Because of the inadequacy of the market place for meeting these demands, the political system becomes increasingly involved in responding to the need for an increase in the level of societal services.

A society with high levels of service confronts both its economic and political system with serious problems. Productivity simply does not increase as rapidly as the cost for services, with the result that inflation is a by-product of a service economy (Bell, 1972). A doctor, teacher, dentist, banker, or travel agent can only handle a certain number of clients within given periods of time. And as the demand for public services increases, expenditures for education, welfare service, police, and the like increase with inflationary results for the entire economy. This, of course, places considerable strain on the government, for it must attempt to control inflation at the same time that it is confronted with demands for more services.

SOCIAL MOBILITY AND SOCIAL STRATIFICATION

Stratification systems in countries with high levels of industrialization have much more in common with one another than do systems in countries with low levels of economic development. While the stratification systems of highly developed societies reach their present condition by many routes, there are, as development takes place, some common processes at work. As the level of industrialization rises, productivity per worker increases, bringing about a smaller proportion of the population in agriculture and a more differentiated occupational structure.

Of course, there are no linear and permanent laws involving changes in social status, the indicators of which are income and wealth, prestige, and power. However, there is substantial evidence to support the view that in the early stages of development, inequality in income and wealth tends to grow, and, at higher levels, equality in income becomes a bit more pervasive and the standard of living for the entire population rises. In countries or areas of lower economic development, extreme concentration of wealth is generally believed necessary for the capital formation required for development. Income distribution is bimodal, with the mean, median, and mode far apart. Once economic development is well under way, however, there is a trend toward a unimodal distribution of income (Kuznets, 1955).

There are several long-term trends at work which help to explain the widening inequality in the early developmental process and a narrowing at later stages. In the early stages of development, there is considerable migration to urban areas, frequently resulting in temporary social disorganization for many groups. Simultaneously, there is a drop in death rates, though fertility rates remain relatively static, but high. Socially and politically disorganized, the population of lower-income groups expands rapidly, with a resulting low per capita income. As economic growth occurs, however, income and wealth become concentrated among those at the top.

In time, however, not only does social cohesion increase among lower-income groups but fertility rates also drop. While this kind of demographic shift improves per capita income, political factors help to bring about modest rearrangements in income distribution. For example, lower-income groups acquire increased political power that is ultimately transmuted into certain legislative decisions—i.e., the passage of progressive taxation and social welfare legislation (Kuznets, 1955).

More important, expanding technology brings about increases in labor productivity and wages. But increases in the level of technology require higher levels of skills within the work force, which causes the society to place considerable emphasis on education. Not only is education provided to all strata of the society, but at high levels of development, education becomes the single most important variable in shaping occupation and social status. And a society with universal education has a stratification system which is relatively open and "merito-cratic."

In order to maintain economic and political stability, members of the population as a whole must increasingly enjoy high standards of living, supplying the mass markets to which production is geared. Largely for these reasons, highly indus-trialized societies have tendencies not only toward a structural egalitarianism, but also toward an egalitarian ideology. Just as this ideology influences changes in the economy, economic growth in turn strengthens the egalitarian ideology.

Despite the difficulty of obtaining precise data on income distribution, several scholarly studies—each conducted sepa-rately and focusing on different societies—reveal that the trend described above is very pronounced. In nonsocialist agrarian societies of the past, the top 2% of the population normally received approximately half the income, whereas, in such highly industrialized societies as the United Kingdom, the United States, Denmark, and Sweden, the same size group received approximately 10% of the income (Lenski, 1966). Analyzing the contemporary world at different levels of economic development, Simon Kuznets (1963) reports, with cross-sectional data, that the top 5% of the population received 65% of all income in Southern Rhodesia, approximately 40% in Mexico and Columbia and 20% in the highly industrial countries of North America and Western Europe. Or one may examine the distribution of income over time within the same country and observe the same kind of trend. In the United States, the top 5% of the population received 31% of income in 1929 and 15% in 1968, while in Great Britain the same elite groups received 46% in 1880, 43% in 1919, 33% in 1929, and 18% in 1967 (Miller, 1971).

In highly developed societies, "white-collar" occupations expand considerably, and "middle-class values" increasingly permeate the entire social structure—though they are not spread evenly throughout the system. Or to phrase it differently, the life styles of the population of a highly industrial society do not vary as much from one level of the stratification system to another, as is the case in a society with a low level of economic development. There is a distinct trend toward a homogeneous style of living.

As the social structure becomes somewhat more diamond-shaped, social classes tend to disappear in the middle strata. And much of the fluidity in a highly industrial society results not so much in upward and downward mobility as it does in lateral mobility in the middle strata.

In a well-known study, Lipset and Zetterberg (1956) reported that Western industrial societies have very similar rates of intergenerational mobility and their stratification systems are relatively immune to religious, ideological, or cultural factors. In a later study, S. M. Miller (1960) demonstrated that, while rates of mobility may not vary, the range of mobility varies considerably in highly industrial societies. In some, mobility involving fairly large changes in status is possible; in other countries, most changes in status are modest.

Even though the life style of the total population becomes more homogeneous in a highly industrial society, distinct status differentials persist. And while there is a narrowing of income and educational differentials between skilled workers and the lower grades of white-collar workers, several studies reveal that these two groups still have different attitudes on many aspects of society. Religion, ethnicity, income and wealth, occupation, level of education, membership in informal and formal organizations, and leisure habits are only a few characteristics that continue to mark status distinctions.

Moreover, wealth in the personal sector of highly industrialized societies seems not to be as equitably distributed as income. For example, the top 1% of adults in the United States held 32% of the wealth in the personal sector in 1922 and 24% in 1953 (Lampman, 1962). And, in British society, 1% of the population in 1911 owned 65% of the wealth, though this had declined by the late 1940s to approximately 35% (Lydall and Tipping, 1961).

Though there is a broad trend toward a somewhat more equitable distribution of both income and wealth as a society moves from a preindustrial to an industrial level, there is no reason to assume that this egalitarianism goes beyond a certain point. In the history of Western industrial societies, it appears that the trend is checked at some point, with the result that considerable inequality of wealth and income remain. And insofar as there is a trend toward less concentration of *personal* resources in highly developed countries, it may well be those in the middle level, not at the bottom, who benefit most by redistributive measures. For unskilled and migrant workers at the bottom, prospects are poor for intergenerational and intragenerational mobility.

Even though our knowledge about rates of mobility is quite imperfect, we do have much better information about the changing elite structure in industrializing societies. At relatively low levels of economic development, economic and political power are closely associated with one's economic resources, while in highly industrial societies, an individual's economic and political power is more closely related to his institutional connections. For example, elites in the economic sphere are also the social and political elites in societies with relatively low levels of economic development. (This is not the case in many multiethnic societies, where certain ethnic groups hold elite positions in one sector but are denied elite positions in other sectors—i.e., Asians in East Africa, Chinese in Malaysia, and Jews in many lands.)

At a high level of development, the economic organization of a society is not compatible with a homogeneous elite group which dominates all sectors of society. Highly industrial societies have considerable bureaucratization and occupational differentiation which cannot tolerate an elite recruitment confined to any particular class or group. Advanced industrial development demands professionally oriented elites based on competence, education, and training rather than family, community, or religious ties.

All elites in highly industrial societies do not acquire their positions on the basis of achievement criteria, however. Indeed, it is useful to draw a distinction between two types of elites: (a) a social elite which is recruited on the basis of wealth and birth and which sets standards of etiquette and life style, and (b) strategic elites who manage a society's complex organizations, people who have a relatively short tenure, and whose authority extends over a narrow area of society. While there may be some overlap between social and strategic elites, they generally constitute two different elite groups (Keller, 1963).

POLITICAL CULTURE

As the economy shifts the stratification system to a diamond-shaped one, the political culture of the society begins to change. Reflecting the attitudes and orientations which individuals have toward the political system, political culture refers to the psychological dimensions of politics, to how governments ought to be conducted and to what government should do.

We might think of two kinds of political culture, at opposite ends of a continuum. At one extreme is a traditional political culture, and at the other is a legal-rational culture. Elements of both types are to be found in most every community, though some political systems have essentially a traditional political culture and others a legal-rational one. For example, the traditional political culture is most likely to be dominant in a society with a low level of economic development and a pyramidal social structure, while the legal-rational political culture is more closely associated with a high level of economic development and a diamond-shaped social structure.

People in a traditional political culture not only feel little obligation to participate in the political process, but they have very little concern with how policy is made. There is, however, much more concern with the way policies affect individuals, or the downward flow of power. Among those who share the traditional political culture, there is considerable cynicism toward the political system, supported by the belief that decisions are made on the basis of particularistic and ascriptive-type criteria.

There is also a tendency to view politics as a dirty business. In general, there is a low commitment to or expectation of honesty in government. And indeed most of those who participate in a political system, which is imbedded in a traditional type of political culture, do so primarily to promote private interests and their own advancement. There is little effort to professionalize or bureaucratize the political process, for this would interfere with the use of personal influence. There is a widely held view that the role of government should be limited, for, if its scope were expanded, this would create opportunities for an increased level of corruption. Moreover, there is very little expectation that government will undertake policies which are designed to benefit the public interest. Rather, there is a widely shared belief that the public benefits only as the unintended consequence of actions by selfish groups of political elites.

The various components of a legal-rational political culture are at the opposite end of the continuum on each of these variables. Among those who share the legal-rational culture, there is a strongly held view that it is their duty to participate in politics. Moreover, they have a high sense of efficacy—that is, the belief that they can influence the political system. There is also a high expectation that people will be recruited to political positions on the basis of demonstrated achievement and competence. And while recruitment on the basis of ascriptive criteria occurs to some extent in any political system, there nevertheless is a belief that people should not be recruited primarily on the basis of religion, race, ethnicity, and family connections.

Concerned very much with considerations of efficiency, economy, and innovation in government services, legal-rationalists advocate systematic and detailed planning in allocating resources and in the solving of community problems. Related to the emphasis on planning is a willingness to have professionals involved in making community decisions—especially in areas involving public health, education, and safety. While informal agreements are necessary in any political system, there is a willingness to use the police, litigation, the courts, and other public agencies to reach formal agreements in solving public conflicts. Bureaucratization is accepted as a means of promoting a higher level of professionalization, efficiency, and formal communication.

In a legal-rational political culture, strains and contradictions emerge as the result of the interaction of participation on the one hand, and professionalization and bureaucratization on the other. In a highly developed society, the population becomes increasingly politicized, and demands for equality and social rights continue to rise: the rights of women, school children, the poor, racial and ethnic minority groups. Demands for more and more public services are made. To cope with demands, the scale of governmental activities increases, political roles become more differentiated, and the size and complexity of bureaucracies increase. In the process, the norms of bureaucratization begin to prevail throughout the political system.

But the emphasis on egalitarianism and individual participation in shaping community decisions often clashes with increased professionalism and bureaucratization. Bureaucratization tends to insulate elites, shrouding their activities in a great deal of secrecy. Within bureaucracies, professionals tend to be more concerned with the opinions of their colleagues in other communities, even other countries, rather than with the attitudes of their clients. Moreover, the norms of professionalization require that decisions be made according to professional standards—which may run contrary to popular opinion. Professionalism of administrators and a kind of populism clash, as the desire for participation reacts to "technocratic" decision-making (Alford, 1969).

These tensions become particularly acute when ethnic minorities make demands which frequently subordinate professional qualifications to ascriptive and particularistic criteria: witness the Catholics of Northern Ireland and Blacks in the United States.

POLITICAL STRUCTURE

In the history of Western democracies, political parties have been one of the major structures performing functions of government. But as the level of economic development has increased, the institutionalization of parties has declined, and many of the functions of government have shifted to other institutions.

As the level of economic development increases, important changes take place in the relationship among parties, interest groups, bureaucracies, and legislatures. Most importantly, parties and legislatures decline in power relative to the role of large organized pressure groups and bureaucracies. These tendencies are manifest in all highly industrial societies, though they are modified according to the structure and role of the central government. In the highly centralized French system, the problems of dispersal and fragmentation of power have obviously been much less severe than in the United States, an extreme example of decentralization and fragmentation.

In contrast to most European social systems, the most important thing to keep in mind when studying political change in American history is that the Americans in their early history confronted no feudal society, no entrenched religious system, no encrusted and rigid social structure. Where these circumstances occurred in Europe, centralization of political authority was usually necessary in order to break down traditional society and to develop a modern one. In contrast, the Americans were able to develop a modern society without a centralized political system, and it is the decentralized character of the American political system that has been its most distinctive and important feature.

In response to a fragmented, decentralized, and diffused political system, the American party system grew up, and, throughout most of the nineteenth century, the party system performed most of the functions of a political system. As party organization has weakened in the twentieth century, political authority has again become extremely dispersed and fragmented.

The decline in the institutionalization of parties and the retreat of parliamentary government does not occur dramatically or suddenly in the industrializing process. Rather, there is a gradual transfer of power and functions into the hands of technical experts. As the government apparatus becomes more complex and the level of services increases, the number of governmental agencies multiply. Functions of government are channeled to government agencies, which in theory are subordinate to either or both executive and legislature, but in fact the machinery of government tends to become increasingly independent of elected officials. Overall, the power of government constantly expands, but as power is increasingly fragmented and dispersed, it is not sufficiently concentrated or centralized for any institution, agency, or any one person to govern a highly industrial society.

In this complicated process, one of the most significant changes involves the relationship between public and private centers of power. For example, bureaucrats find it necessary to consult with organized pressure groups for information and cooperation, and in some instances, the relationship between private and public governments becomes so intricate that the government agency is coopted or colonized by powerfully organized interest groups.

This tendency is very apparent in the relationship between American regulatory agencies and pressure groups. Relatively isolated from the White House and Congress, many regulatory agencies have developed their own constituencies—frequently the very industry which they are to regulate. As intimate relations develop between regulatory agencies and industry, the political process becomes increasingly one of self-governing estates within the federal structure, one in which numerous major interests are able to shape public policy by what in essence amounts to a delegation of national sovereignty to private governments (Lowi, 1969).

Because the officials of most government agencies are appointed, elections offer little opportunity for the public to choose or decide among competing policies. Elections, however, do tend to legitimate the "technocracy process," frequently giving the public the illusion that it is vitally involved in the political process.

Of course, elected officials still exercise considerable influence in the political process, and one must not exaggerate the extent to which power has been parcelled out to governmental agencies. Legislatures, for example, do retain considerable power over budgets, a factor of immense importance in influencing certain policies.

While the power of the executive branch of government expands in societies with high levels of industrialization, the executive branch becomes seriously confronted with problems of fractionalization and compartmentalization. No chief executive has the time or knowledge to comprehend the actions of all agencies of the executive branch, with the result that there is diffusion of information, and, consequently, authority.

Built into most government bureaucracies is a skepticism of planned change, a desire to preserve the status quo, a bias for precedent and the familiar, a predisposition toward the compromising of diverse opinions, a dislike of experiments, abstractions, and untried policies. And even if a minister of chief executive succeeds in overhauling a government bureaucracy, the effect is likely to be only temporary—for the civil servants will again return to their world of anonymity, secrecy, and routine.

In the American political system, fragmentation of power exists at all levels of government. Below the national level, power is dispersed among fifty states and over 80,000 local governments. In some metropolitan areas, there are literally dozens of "governments." Some years ago, Robert Wood (1961) counted 1,400 governments in the metropolitan area of New York City. For the smaller area around Chicago, there were, in 1960, 1,060 governments, 995 of which had the power to raise taxes. Functions involving land-use patterns, transportation, health, water, and air pollution are shared by so many agencies that a coherent policy for metropolitan areas is a virtual impossibility. At the state level, the fragmentation of authority by quasi-autonomous agencies, many effectively reponsible only to narrow constituencies, has also meant that public policy is shaped very much by private groups which effectively penetrate the government bureaucracy (Lowi, 1969).

Because the American system has historically been relatively decentralized and because it has a higher level of industrialization than any other country, the diffusion and fragmentation of authority in the American political system has been carried to greater extremes than in any other society. It is the success with which interest groups have penetrated the government and the vast power that they exert in shaping public policy that led Andrew Hacker to remark that the "United States has as powerless a government as any developed nation in the modern world" (Hacker, 1970).

Modernization has brought about two counter-tendencies. On the one hand, it has led to government by the trained expert, the specialist, and to a decline in power of elected officials and political parties. Industrial . societies are composed of giant corporations in labor, industry, government, and education. And in each sector as the individual has yielded to the power of the large-scale organization, he has felt increasingly helpless to influence societal decision-making. On the other hand, modernization has provided the social conditions which have increased the politicization of and demands for participation by mass publics. As voters have been uprooted by industrialization, free of a stable class structure and increasingly deprived of both meaningful primary group association and well-institutionalized political parties, the mass base of politics has become somewhat volatile.

Thus, the problem of maintaining a society with commonly shared values has become one of the most critical challenges facing political elites. A high level of modernization has meant an erosion of traditional values of status, prestige, and morality. And with the weakening of traditional institutions and values, political elites have increasingly found it difficult to engage in a symbolic activity which will develop—or maintain—a societal consensus on major issues of the day.

PUBLIC POLICY

Societies with low levels of development have very few public institutions which provide services for their citizens. With the level of government services extremely low, the family is the most important institution providing welfare for children, the disabled, and the elderly. Public sewage facilities hardly exist, and the water supply is inadequate. Disease is widespread, and the mortality rate is very high.

As the level of economic development increases, people demand better living conditions as they become able to purchase more than the basic requirements for life. For example, English working-class families spent 74% of their income on food in 1794, but only 40% in 1937; and Massachusetts working-class families spent 57% of their income on food in 1874, 40% in 1903, and 34% in 1935 (Stigler, 1956). The demand for services increases with the following: higher levels of technology, higher per capita income, reduced inequality of income, larger proportions of the population who are children and aged, higher levels of education, and urbanization of society (Stigler, 1956). A rising per capita income and the concentration of people in urban areas are especially related to increases in government expenditures involving education, sanitation, transportation, fire, police, and public health. Too, governments become involved in breaking down traditional obstructions to equality of economic opportunity.

While there is no one-to-one relationship between the level of government expenditure and gross national product, there is a tendency for government expenditures to increase as a percentage of GNP as the level of economic development rises. In the contemporary world, Ethiopia and Afghanistan government expenditures are 5% of GNP, India and Pakistan approximately 10%, Greece almost 20%, and West Germany about 33%. And the relationship between expanding governmental activity and increases in the level of economic development is very apparent in American history. For example, all government expenditures were approximately 8% of GNP in 1900, but this had increased to 28% of GNP in 1966 (Eckstein, 1964).

Why do government functions increase and public services expand as the level of economic development rises? Governments rarely lower their tax rates. Hence, a given tax rate yields higher revenues as the economy expands, and expenditures rise in response to increases in revenues. And the higher the level of development, the more numerous and larger the government bureaucracies. Because bureaucracies almost inevitably seek to expand, the increases in revenues are constantly used.

Moreover, Western societies have entered wars, the financing of which has required higher tax levels. Because postwar taxes rarely drop to their previous levels, wars have a permanent effect of driving up revenues and generating an expansion of governmental activities (Eckstein, 1964).

Governments do different things, however. While there are broad similarities in public policies, there are also important divergences at comparable levels of development. And cultural factors are useful in explaining policy differences among political systems (King, 1971).

Despite the vast historical literature which demonstrates the important role which the state played in the economic development of the United States, the Americans, in contrast to the people of Western Europe, have historically preferred a state which is less involved in the affairs of society. Differences in American and European practices are sharply revealed in their approaches to state ownership of enterprises. For example, many European states have substantial or complete ownership of the railways, airlines, telephones, radio and television, electricity, gas, coal, oil, and banking. And while the American government has occasionally undertaken commercial activity, this has usually been done to increase the supply and lower the cost of some good or service. Of course, the American government has long subsidized a variety of economic activities, but most of the economic activity, even when the government has been involved, has been overwhelmingly private.

Despite historical variations in attitudes about the function of government, the process of industrialization does bring about common expectations and demands with regard to public services, and this is especially clear in the area of public welfare. "The higher the average productivity of labor, the more profitable it becomes to extend the effective working life span of the worker and to keep him fully employed" (Rimlinger, 1966: 557). As a result, highly developed societies make substantial investments in health, welfare, and education of their citizens. And while Americans spend substantial private sums of money on welfare services, the government spends a substantially smaller percentage of the national income on welfare than do most governments of Western Europe.

While it is extremely difficult to compare the quality and the extent of social services among political systems, it is useful to note that governments do more in each area of social service the longer their involvement. The highly developed European countries had government-supported old-age pensions, public housing, unemployment insurance, and medical services long before the United States—and this explains, in part, the lag in the nature of American services.

Public education on a mass level is one area in which the Americans became involved earlier than other societies, and therefore it should not be surprising that they have long spent a higher percentage of their GNP on public education and that they have long had a higher percentage of their population in public schools than most other highly developed societies.

In countless areas, there are inadequate private markets to meet the demands of the society, with the result that government functions are constantly expanding. Public housing for low-income families, flood control projects, and inexpensive electric power are only a few examples of policy areas in which governments become involved because the market does not respond to public demands.

As the level of technology increases, costs for certain types of research and development become prohibitive for firms in the private sector. In a highly industrial society, governments become increasingly involved in scientific activity. For example, the central government of the United States in 1960 financed 65% of university research and 57% of private industry research. If innovations for many costly items are to occur, governments either totally or partially underwrite the costs, thus further blurring the lines between public and private governments.

As the level of economic development increases, the escalating demands for governmental activity increase the loads on government to such an extent that the political system's legitimacy suffers. Governmental activities become increasingly visible, involving more and more every segment of society. Decisions about the location of streets and highways, the design and quality of consumer products, the content of school curricula, the quality of air and water, the generation, distribution, and organization of wealth—all of these and countless other issues involving the quality of life are constantly exposing the gap between government performance and public expectations. As the society focuses on the government's shortcomings, demands increase for government to become more active, flexible, and innovative. Government responds by establishing new programs and agencies, thus creating more governmental fragmentation and duplication of programs. But, as power is increasingly dispersed, the government has a diminishing capacity to develop policies in some coordinated and integrated fashion.

CONCLUDING REMARKS

This paper is based on both empirical investigations and historical speculation. The excuse for presenting such an abbreviated conceptual framework, some of which is without sound empirical foundations, is a deep interest in the processes of change in Western industrializing societies and a wish to share this concern with the scholarly community. More importantly, our understanding of these processes is most inadequate, and many of our best empirical studies are not cast within either a comparative or a theoretical framework. Speculating both comparatively and theoretically about structural and cultural changes in Western societies is an effort to channel historical interests and research in these directions. If the reader will view many of the ideas contained herein as tentative statements for further investigation, perhaps this essay will result in little harm and some good.

The next stage in this kind of analysis calls for an explicit model of social change, one which is quite precise in specifying the relationships among the various components of change. Until we move to this level of analysis, our statements about social change, by necessity, will remain oversimplified generalizations. At best, this essay represents only the first step in narrowing the gap between historical investigations and a type of theory construction strongly based in historical analysis.

The tone of this essay suggests that Western societies are moving in a common direction. In this respect, it is important to make a sharp distinction between similarity and difference on the one hand, and, on the other, convergence and divergence. Societies may be different in many respects, but certain structures and cultural attributes may be converging (Dunning and Hopper, 1966). And even though converging processes may be occurring, there may simultaneously be diverging processes. As we become more sophisticated conceptually and methodologically in comparative analysis, and as the quality of time series data improves, perhaps we can eventually be much more explicit about the degree of convergence and divergence, of similarities and differences which industrializing societies encounter.

REFERENCES

ALFORD, R. R. (1969) Bureaucracy and Participation: Political Cultures in Four Wisconsin Cities. Chicago: Rand McNally.

AVERITT, R. T. (1968) The Dual Economy: The Dynamics of American Industry Structure. New York: W. W. Norton.

BELL, D. (1972) "Labour in the post-industrial society." Dissent (Winter): 163-189.

DUNNING, E. G. and E. I. HOPPER (1966) "Industrialization and the problem of convergence: a critical note." Soc. Rev. 14 (July): 163-86.

EASTERLIN, R. A. (1961) "Regional income trends, 1840-1950," in S. Harris (ed.) American Economic History. New York: McGraw-Hill.

ECKSTEIN, O. (1964) Public Finance. Englewood Cliffs, N.J.: Prentice-Hall.

HACKER (1970) The End of the American Era. New York: Atheneum.

HIRSCHMAN, A. O. (1965) The Strategy of Economic Development. New Haven, Conn.: Yale Univ. Press.

KELLER, S. (1963) Beyond the Ruling Class. New York: Random House.

KINDLEBERGER, C. P. (1969) American Business Abroad. New Haven, Conn.: Yale Univ. Press.

KING, A. (1971) "Ideologies as predictors of public policy patterns: a comparative analysis." Presented at Sixty-Seventh Annual Meeting of American Political Science Association, Chicago.

KUZNETS, S. (1963) "Quantitative aspects of the economic growth of nations." Econ. Development and Cultural Change 11 (January): Part 2.

——— (1955) "Economic growth and income inequality." Amer. Econ. Rev. 45 (March): 1-28.

LAMPMAN, R. J. (1962) The Share of Top Wealth-Holders in National Wealth: 1922-1956. Princeton: Princeton Univ. Press.

LENSKI, G. E. (1966) Power and Privilege. New York: McGraw-Hill.

LIPSET, S. M. and H. L. ZETTERBERG (1956) "A theory of social mobility." Transactions of the Third World Congress of Sociology 3: 155-177.

LOWI, T. J. (1969) The End of Liberalism. New York: W. W. Norton.

LYDALL, H. F. and D. G. TIPPING (1961) "The distribution of personal wealth in Britain." Bull. of Oxford University Institute of Economics and Statistics.

MILLER, H. P. (1971) Rich Man, Poor Man. New York: Thomas Y. Crowell.

MILLER, S. M. (1960) "Comparative social mobility." Current Sociology 9, 1: 1-15.

RIMLINGER, G. V. (1966) "Welfare policy and economic development: a comparative historical perspective." J. of Econ. History 26 (December): 556-571.

STIGLER, G. J. (1956) Trends in Employment in the Service Industries. Princeton: Princeton Univ. Press.

WILLIAMSON, J. G. (1965) "Regional inequality and the process of national development: a description of the patterns." Econ. Development and Cultural Change 13: 3-45.

WOOD, R. (1961) 1400 Governments, the Political Economy of the New York Metropolitan Region. Cambridge, Mass.: Harvard Univ. Press.

Group Cohesion and Social and Ideological Conflict

A Critique of Some Marxian and Tocquevillian Theories

LEE BENSON
University of Pennsylvania

As I view the contemporary academic world, a revolutionary crisis exists in history-as-discipline. By revolutionary crisis, I mean that great expectations once inspired its professors. Self-evidently, those expectations remain unfulfilled. As a group, historians have contributed little to the advancement of social thought.[1] We know it. It disturbs us. Increasingly, I am convinced, we recognize that only radical solutions can overcome the general crisis in historiography and thereby help us overcome our *personal* (i.e., professional) crisis.

Granted the correctness of that diagnosis, reorientation and reorganization is the rational remedy. Concretely, my argument is that individuals who want to do good social scientific history, for example, must specialize in *social scientific history,* rather than *history.* I do not say that doing social scientific history is the only legitimate way to do history. On the contrary, I only

Author's Note: *This essay is based partly on research supported by a grant from the National Science Foundation (GS-2879) to test the possibility that selected aspects of past human behavior can serve, in effect, as natural experiments for the development of social scientific theories. The current*

say that to do social scientific history differs radically from other equally legitimate ways to do history.

Granted that argument, to fill my prescription (reorientation and reorganization), I must effectively answer this question: How should social scientific history be organized? Following a brilliant lead provided by Robert Merton (1968: 39-72), I think that, while working toward the overall goal of a unified theory of societal evolution, social scientific historians should *practically* organize themselves around middle-range theoretical fields of specialization. To try now to map, precisely and comprehensively, the universe of middle-range theoretical fields that should constitute the brave new world of social scientific history would be Utopian. Instead, it seems best to begin that process by focusing attention on one field of theoretical specialization that "cries out" for planned, rational, sustained development—namely, theories of group cohesion and social and ideological conflict.[2]

MARX'S GENERAL THEORIES OF HUMAN NATURE AND SOCIETAL EVOLUTION, AND "SPECIAL" THEORY OF SOCIAL CLASS CONFLICT

"The *whole of what is called world history* is nothing but the creation of man by human labour." Committed to that conception of man's self-development through activity to control nature, Marx worked to create a practical theory of social revolution that would help men replace capitalism with communist humanism. To create such a theory and win

members of my graduate and undergraduate seminars in theories of group cohesion and conflict have forcefully helped me to wrestle with the problems considered in this essay. Readers of this essay will notice that some of its key ideas develop leads provided by Robert Merton. In previous writings, I have indicated my heavy intellectual debt to Paul Lazarsfeld and Ernest Nagel. I am delighted that this essay affords an appropriate occasion to indicate that Mr. Merton was one of the trio of great Columbia scholars who, during the 1950s, when I was associated with that university's Bureau of Applied Social Research, helped me get my bearings as I set out to find the road to social scientific history.

credence for it, he needed a general theory of societal evolution. As I read Marx, he logically derived his general theory of societal evolution from his theory of human nature. What is man? A species of social animal, Marx answered, endowed with a *radically unique combination* of universal, immutable physiological needs or "drives" (e.g., food, shelter, sex, sociability) and universal, immutable physiological capacities or "faculties" (e.g., to form groups, to form concepts, to learn from experience, to communicate and educate, to make tools). Given their radically unique endowment, an inherent tendency exists for men consciously to strive to produce their means of subsistence more effectively by inventing new technologies, new institutions (broadly conceived) and new types of societies.[3]

How can we explain concretely both the overall general direction of societal evolution and the different patterns of evolution of specific societies? That problem is the one with which Marx wrestled. To solve it, he sketched the outlines of a dynamic systems theory organized around this proposition:

The complex set of dialectical interactions between men's universal physiological needs and potential capacities functions as the driving force of the historical development of humanity.[4]

Physiological necessity is the mother of technological and institutional invention. More precisely, Marx theorized, physiological necessity sometimes in some places is the mother of technological and institutional invention (broadly conceived to comprehend forms of social interaction, formal organizations, ideational patterns). When? Where? How? Why?

To use reified language, Marx's complex answers can be (too) simply summarized as follows:

General societal evolution, as well as the evolution of particular societies, both result from conflicts among technologies, institutions, and societies. Over time, the technologies, institutions, and societies that win the struggle for existence satisfy this requirement: more effectively than competitors, they help men realize (in all senses) their inherent potential capacities to satisfy their physiological needs (in the different forms that universal physiological needs take in different societies). Given their inherent sociability, common antagonist (Nature), and compelling superordinate goal (increased productive capacity), men inherently need to abolish social and ideological conflict. But they can realize that need effectively only at a highly developed stage of societal evolution. Human history, therefore, is the process whereby men continually struggle to create new technologies and institutions that eventually will enable them to create a radically new type of society in which, for the first time, they can be truly human.

As my summary of Marx's theory of societal evolution is designed to suggest, I do not believe it is best viewed as a class-based theory of social revolution in capitalist societies. Instead, it is best viewed as a broadly humanist theory of *the historical evolution and abolition of social and ideological conflict.*

In contrast to Marx's general theories of human nature and societal evolution, I believe that most of his special or lower-level theories have serious weaknesses and do not fully derive from his general theories. To a significant extent, they tend to derive from the economic determinist notions that, in a post-French Revolutionary era of economic development, he understandably, but uncritically, took over from the "bourgeois economists," St. Simonians, and French "bourgeois historians" who had "discovered" the class struggle in history. For our present purposes, of course, the relevant lower-level theory is his theory of group cohesion and social and ideological conflict. (In this context, "group" and "social" refer to relatively large groups.)

To be more precise, as I read Marx, he did not advance a single, coherent theory of group cohesion and social and ideological conflict. Instead, he advanced two ambiguously formulated, radically different theories. To evaluate them, we must first disentangle and identify them.

MARX'S SOCIAL CLASS CONFLICT THEORY

To identify what I regard as Marx's potentially most comprehensive and credible theory of conflict and cohesion, I label it his *mode of production theory* (sketched below). Unfortunately, in my judgment, he and Engels badly mixed it up with his *social class conflict theory*—a theory that, ironically, fits precapitalist societies better than it does the modern capitalist societies whose demise they thought it would speed (Marx, 1963a: 9-10).

Space prevents a detailed critique of the theory that Marx and Engels, "un-Marxianly," in my judgment, deemed equally applicable to conflict and to cohesion in precapitalist, as well as capitalist, societies. But the main thrust of my critique can be outlined as follows:

(1) The theory essentially is economic determinist in character; it derives from the arbitrary, unrealistic assumption that economic attributes are the only real social attributes.

(2) It essentially disregards Marx's recognition that economic class and social class are radically different concepts and refer to radically different, but related, phenomena. His critical theoretical problem, therefore, was to identify and give relative weights to the different conditions under which the *nominal members of a demographic group* (economic class) do and do not strongly tend to function as *conscious members of a communal group* (social class).

(3) It essentially disregards the radical differences between, to quote Marx (italics in original), distinctions of "birth, social rank, education, occupation" when politically established by formal law and the same types of distinctions when they "are *non-political* distinctions; when . . . [the political state] proclaims, without regard to these distinctions, that every member of society is an *equal* partner in popular sovereignty."

(4) It does not derive from the dynamic systems theory of society whose outlines Marx partially succeeded in envisioning and sketching. Instead, it derives from the antidialectical, mechanical, materialist element in his thinking that led him to use perhaps the most unfortunate metaphor in the history of social thought

—namely, the "foundation-superstructure" metaphor that continues to plague Marxian social theorists.

An ambiguous term, "economic determinism" encompasses at least four different concepts. Disentangling and identifying them helps us to understand how Marx and Engels could criticize some variants and still postulate an essentially economic determinist theory of social and ideological conflict. As is well known, Marx dismissed pocketbook, interest group economic determinism. That is, he dismissed as "'vulgar' common sense" the egoistic notion that similar economic attributes automatically bind individuals together by motivating them to consciously calculate their interests, develop ideas favorable to their interests, engage in conflicts "good" for their interests (Bottomore and Rubel, 1964: 201-202). In like manner, Engels dismissed "as an excuse for *not* studying history" (Marx and Engels, 1942: 472-475, 516-519) what elsewhere I have characterized as the antihistorical, invariant law version of economic determinism. It holds that, irrespective of time, place, or history, similar economic conditions produce men who think and behave similarly (Benson, 1960: 97-100). Giving full weight to their strictures against those variants, it seems indisputable that Marx and Engels developed less "vulgar" and more historical variants of economic determinism.

From Marx's general theory that man as a species continually produces himself (i.e., transforms himself) in the process of trying to produce his means of subsistence more effectively, he unwarrantedly derived a proposition that he treated as self-evidently true: in any society, for the vast majority of individuals, economic attributes function as the only *real* social attributes. No other type of attribute forms a real basis for social groups. In all societies, at all stages of societal evolution, these equations must be true: (1) economic existence = social existence; (2) economic structure = social structure (Marx, 1963a: 46-47).

To appreciate how narrowly Marx viewed social reality when he theorized about it, we need only recognize that he permitted the *relations of production* to loom so large in his vision as to block out his awareness that the relations of *re*production also form a material part of social reality. More broadly, when we fully appreciate the economic determinist character of his conception of social reality, I think we understand better why, in effect, he unwarrantedly dismissed ethnic, religious, and national attributes (among others) as not real elements of it (Struik, 1971: 109).

The fourth concept of economic determinism noted here derives from the third sketched above. But it is subtly, significantly different. It can be identified by quoting one of Marx's most sweeping (and ambiguous) propositions: "It is not the consciousness of men that determines their existence, but, on the contrary, their social existence determines their consciousness" (Feuer, 1959: 43). Given his economic determinist conception of social existence, that proposition asserts that in all societies this syllogism is true:

(1) Present economic existence (class) = social existence.

(2) Social existence = consciousness.

(3) Therefore, present economic existence (class) = consciousness.

Critically examined, that syllogism is both radically anti-historical and demonstrably contrary to empirical reality. It is, therefore, in my judgment, radically "un-Marxian."

Marx's Mode of Production Theory

Space permits me only to sketch in skeletal outline the potentially powerful mode-of-production theory of group cohesion and social and ideological conflict that can be developed from Marx's general theory of societal evolution and numerous brilliant but scattered observations. As I formulate it (in desperately abbreviated form), the theory asserts:

(1) The past and present modes of production of a society strongly tend to determine the general parameters and nature of its past and present patterns of intrasocietal conflict *and cooperation*.

(2) The past and present modes of production of a society significantly tend to determine the general parameters and nature of past and present patterns of intersocietal conflict and cooperation.

(3) Significant reciprocal relationships strongly tend to exist between a society's intrasocietal and intersocietal patterns of conflict and cooperation.

A brief quotation from Marx (1963b: 115) adds flesh to the bare-bone skeleton above:

Each principle has had its own century in which to manifest itself. The principle of authority, for example, had the eleventh century, just as the principle of individualism had the eighteenth century. . . . When . . . we ask ourselves why a particular principle was manifested in the eleventh or in the eighteenth century rather than in any other, we are necessarily forced to examine minutely what men were like in the eleventh century, what they were like in the eighteenth, what were their respective needs, their productive forces, their mode of production, the raw materials of their production—in short, what were the relations between man and man which resulted from all these conditions of existence.

As noted earlier, Marx viewed conditions of existence through economic determinist spectacles. But to mix metaphors shamelessly, if we do not look through his spectacles but stand on his shoulders, we can see more clearly than he was able to see. For example, his general mode of production theory then permits us to advance specific claims of this type:

As a result of complex processes primarily caused by the historical development of the modes of production of Western European societies after 1500, ethnocultural and religious heterogeneity of an unprecedented, unparalleled kind characterized mid-nineteenth-century American society. In that society, the combined *alienating* effects of past and present modes of production functioned as the main underlying cause (or condition) of antagonistic relationships. But ethnocultural and religious attributes, not economic attributes, mainly functioned as the concrete bases of group cohesion and social and ideological conflict.

In more general terms, as I formulate Marx's mode of production theory of cohesion and conflict, it asserts three basic propositions:

(1) In any society, if private ownership of the means of production, then, at minimum, significant social and ideological conflict. (The specific form or forms are determined by a complex set of variables, including history and contemporary intersocietal relations.)

(2) Taking *networks* of significantly interacting societies as the unit of analysis, if private ownership of the means of production and advanced industrial development, then, at minimum, high levels of violent and nonviolent social and ideological conflict. (The specific form or forms are determined by a complex set of variables, including history and contemporary intersocietal relations.)

(3) Taking the *dominant* world societies as the unit of analysis, if common ownership of the means of production and highly developed systems of science and technology, then, after some period of transition from precommunist modes of production, no significant social conflict, ideological conflict, or violence.

As hinted above, Marx's mode of production theory can logically be extended to encompass patterns of cooperation, as well as patterns of conflict. Again following a brilliant lead provided by Robert Merton (1968: 278-440), I think Marx's theory can also be further extended to function as the materialist core of a powerful upper-middle-range theory —namely, the theory of reference group determination of behavior—a body of theory whose development holds particularly great potential power for students of heterogeneous societies (e.g., the United States).

The economic determinist strain in Marx's thought led him to detract from what I have termed his mode of production theory by entangling it in his social class theory. For present purposes, it is particularly critical to emphasize that his social class theory rests on two unwarranted assumptions:

(1) except for a relatively small proportion of highly deviant individuals, men's orientations primarily derive from their membership in a specific social class;

(2) men can orient themselves only negatively to members of other social classes.

In direct contrast, reference group theory provides these great advantages: (1) it recognizes that noneconomic, as well as economic, attributes can function as significant, real bases of social groups from which men derive both their positive and negative orientations; (2) it aims to "account for *both* membership- and non-membership-group [positive and negative] orientations [to groups and individuals]" (Merton, 1968: 288). The potential inherent in Marx's mode of production theory of cohesion and conflict unfortunately has tended to remain undeveloped—in large part because he entangled and equated it with his social class theory. And that confusion occurred largely because of the economic determinist climate of opinion in which Marx and Engels developed their ideas. Simply at face value, that belief seems reasonable. But it gains greater credence when we recognize that their contemporary, Alexis de Tocqueville, also developed an economic determinist theory of group cohesion and social and ideological conflict.

DE TOCQUEVILLE'S STATUS THEORY OF GROUP COHESION AND SOCIAL AND IDEOLOGICAL CONFLICT

De Tocqueville, unlike Marx, had no general theory of societal evolution, other than "the will of God." (One reason that de Tocqueville ranks much below Marx as a social theorist is that Marx's theory of societal evolution is immeasurably superior to de Tocqueville's [1966: 3-14] "providential" explanation of the coming of the "democratic revolution" after 1100.) Like Marx, however, de Tocqueville derived his theory of cohesion and conflict from his theory of human nature (as, in fact, all social theorists do—and must). Space again dictates an oversimplified, summary sketch.

Viewed in historical perspective, de Tocqueville's theory of human nature represents an updated variant of ancient elitist notions (e.g., "master people," "natural aristocracies," divinely-blessed "elects"). In his version of elitist theory, human nature has two main attributes, one variable, the other constant:

(1) In all societies, at all times, an inherent radical inequality exists in the distribution of talent and virtue.

(2) In all societies, at all times, all men inherently have an equally powerful "instinctive love" for equality, an equally powerful "passion for equality" of status—i.e., a passion to rank *beneath* no one else in prestige, public honor, public esteem. (The second attribute seems to be de Tocqueville's original contribution to elitist theories of human nature—a contribution that could credibly be explained by applying a theory of ideology derived from Marx.)[5]

From his theory of human nature, de Tocqueville derived what recently has become an influential theory of cohesion and conflict in modern societies. In societies that enjoy legal inequality of status conditions, he theorized, the inherent passion for equality tends strongly to be suppressed. In such societies, men can only be who the law says they must be. Therefore, they know who they are. Within and even between orders or estates, genuine affective social relationships are possible and actually tend to exist. Status is fixed. Conflicts over status, therefore, cannot significantly disturb the social order, and great achievements are possible. To quote de Tocqueville (1966: 8), "The body social thus ordered could lay claim to stability, strength, and above all, glory."

But in Christian societies (de Tocqueville here seems to anticipate Weber's criticism of Marx by emphasizing the role of values derived from religious doctrines), God chose to bring about an "irresistible revolution" that inevitably must result in complete equality of legal status (de Tocqueville, 1966: 6, 10). In societies not ordered by legal inequality, de Tocqueville theorized, the passion for equality cannot be suppressed; it then functions as the driving force of group cohesion (inevitably limited) and social and ideological conflict (strongly tending to be widespread and fierce).

For de Tocqueville, it was literally inconceivable that societies could exist without marked inequalities of wealth—i.e., without something like upper, middle, and lower economic classes. Equality of legal status conditions unleashes passions and energies and movements to bring about equality of nonlegal status conditions. But no significant movement could develop that aimed to bring about equality of wealth. Thus, conflicts center on status, not wealth.

When legally equal to all other men, no man can be sure who he is, who he will be, or with whom he will permanently associate. As a result, driven by their instinctive, insatiable passion for status equality, all men find themselves trapped in a never-ending struggle for status honor. Given the natural inequality of human beings, it follows that "the weak . . . want to drag the strong down to their level and . . . men . . . prefer equality in servitude to inequality in freedom" (de Tocqueville, 1966: 49).

In a society characterized by legal equality and laws of inheritance that tend toward the "equal sharing of a father's property among his children," who are the weak and who are the "strong?" That question does not seem to have been clearly answered by de Tocqueville. In effect, however, he invoked something like the Calvinist doctrine of election and positively associated strength (i.e., intellect and virtue) with wealth.

Differential wealth gives individuals differential power to acquire the things that increase (or preserve) status honor. Thus, one form of the fierce battle for status is a fierce battle for money. But in "democratic" societies, money does not primarily function as an end in itself, or as a means to secure material goods and services. In such societies, money primarily functions to secure the things that an individual can use to increase his status honor compared to all other individuals, including other "members" of his economic class. Thus the rich men—presumptively, the "natural aristocrats"—fiercely struggle with one another.

De Tocqueville, like Marx, emphasized that rich men do have an overriding common interest that should link them together, despite their egoistic competition. (Unlike Marx, however, he thought it problematic that rich men actually would link themselves together—in the absence of theorists like de Tocqueville. What Marx wanted to do for the proleteriat, de Tocqueville wanted to do for the rich men.) Because men are rich, they can and do tend to acquire the things that yield high status. The rich serve, therefore, as targets of the nonrich, enviously, passionately driven to abolish all social distinctions based on and manifested in value systems, cultural achievements, and life styles. For de Tocqueville, whom I view as the self-appointed theorist of the counter-revolution against the levelling effects of the "democratic revolution," the nonrich in democratic societies, uncontrolled, must function as cultural Luddites, cultural institution breakers.

De Tocqueville did not clearly specify the different strata in the status systems of democratic societies (America, of course, only served as the prototype). But he seems to have conceived them as roughly coinciding with the three economic classes (rich, middle, poor). Relative to other strata, the members of each stratum have common interests. The rich try to preserve their status from the levelling attacks of the nonrich; the middle stratum fights a two-front war against rich and poor; the poor try to pull down to their debased level the middle and rich strata.

As I read de Tocqueville, he postulated an essentially Social Darwinist theory of cohesion and conflict in modern societies that were fated to endure legal equality of status conditions. That "social state" inevitably produced conditions that might lead to a Hobbesian war of all against all, each distrusting the other and all passionately desiring status honor. But the members of each stratum (particularly the rich), while egoistically struggling against each other, alternatively might constitute an interest group vis-à-vis the members of other strata (Nisbet, 1966: 179-193).

To evaluate and develop fruitful theories of cohesion and

conflict, I think it necessary to develop a general typology of social groups based on the criterion, degree of communality. (As I conceive communality, it actually is an index with four components: patterned interaction, similarity of interests, similarity of ideational patterns, consciousness of kind.) On the (optimistic) assumption that the terms convey its essence, in barest outline, I sketch a tripartite typology ordered in ascending degree of communality: (1) interest or associational group; (2) quasi-communal group; (3) communal group.

Using that typology, de Tocqueville's theory of cohesion and conflict in "democratic" societies can be seen to be economic determinist in character. He postulated neither a wholly Hobbesian atomistic world of men in a state of nature from which Leviathan rescues them, nor a Marxian world of men engaged in fierce economic conflicts that lead them to create communal groups in the form of social classes. Instead, he postulated a world in which the members of status strata based on wealth tend to function as interest groups.

For de Tocqueville, like Marx, economic attributes are the only real attributes. If laws did not naturally, as it were, group men together by assigning them fixed positions in the economic structure of a society, he could not conceive of the existence of communal groups based on, for example, ethnic, religious, or other noneconomic attributes: no fixed legal relations of production, no quasi-communal or communal groups. That is de Tocqueville's iron law of social groups in noncapitalist and capitalist societies. Hence, his tremendous emphasis on the need for elites (i.e., "the most powerful, intelligent and moral classes") in capitalist societies to act unitedly and wisely to channel and control the fierce struggle for status honor. To do so, they must create political systems and voluntary associational systems firmly controlled by pluralistic elites (not democrats). As the quotation below suggests, de Tocqueville's (1945: vol. 2; 109-110) policy theory derived directly from his empirical and normative theories:

> [Quasi-communal or communal] influences are almost null in democratic countries, they must therefore be artificially created, and

this can only be accomplished by associations. . . . Among the laws that rule human societies there is one which seems to be more precise and clear than all others. If men are to remain civilized or to become so, the art of associating together must grow and improve in the same ratio in which the equality of [legal] conditions is increased.

PROPOSITIONS DERIVED FROM A COMBINED, EXTENDED, MARXIAN-TOCQUEVILLIAN THEORY OF GROUP COHESION AND SOCIAL AND IDEOLOGICAL CONFLICT

Having sketched in skeletal outline a critique of Marx's and de Tocqueville's theories, I turn now to American historiography. In compressed form, this is my argument: crude, simplistic variants of Marx's and de Tocqueville's theories have dominated American historiography since Turner began the Americanization of Marx in the 1890s.[6] More precisely: to the extent that American historians have used theory to help them explain group cohesion and social and ideological conflict, they have tended overwhelmingly to draw (more or less consciously) upon Americanized (and vulgarized) variants of Marx and de Tocqueville.

The Tocquevillian influence in American historiography, of course, is a post-World-War-II happening. Characterized (and slightly caricatured) in a sentence, it has manifested itself in the protean form of free-floating status-anxiety and status-deprivation explanations of wildly diverse and frequently contradictory sets of phenomena (e.g., abolitionism and anti-abolitionism, radical leftism and radical rightism).

From Marx—by way of Turner and Beard (and reaching its ultimate oversimplification in Arthur Schlesinger, Jr. [1945: 307 n.3, 18-29, 505-523 and throughout])—American historians took economic interest as the all-purpose explanatory formula. From de Tocqueville—by way of Riesman, Lipset, Bell, et al.—they took status-anxiety and status-deprivation as a somewhat more restricted, but still sweeping, explanatory formula (Nisbet, 1966: 179-182; de Tocqueville, 1966: III-XXIII). And sometimes they combined both formulas.

From the mid-1950s on, a growing body of empirical research has been published that more or less directly challenges the simplistic variants of Marx that Turner and Beard in their "Progressive" innocence and "New History" zeal had smuggled into American historiography (Bogue, 1968; Swierenga, 1971; Formisano, 1971). Among other things, the anti-Turnerian-Beardian research was designed to suggest that, when "native American radicalism" is viewed in comparative perspective, (i.e., to radicalism in other societies), it becomes clear that Turner and Beard (and Parrington) had ideologically inflated relatively minor, limited, transitory economic interest group fights into profoundly ideological, enduring "class struggles in America." But economic determinism of the pocketbook, petit bourgeois-type, dies hard; more precisely, it dies hard in American historiography.

As might be expected, after it was "discovered" in the early 1960s that American "progress" had not really abolished poverty, it was also discovered that conflict really had always existed in America. (Anti-economic determinists, of course, had emphasized that fierce conflicts existed. They had shown, however, that American social and ideological conflicts were not primarily based on economic attributes and could by no "progressive" stretch of the imagination be considered "class struggles.") And, as might be expected in the decade of the "New Frontier" and "New Left," economic determinism was resurrected from the intellectual graveyard to which wishful thinkers (like myself) had consigned it and thought it safely buried (Benson, 1972: 3-80, 1961, 1960). To distinguish 1960s version from Turner-Beard-Parrington Old Progressivism, yet indicate ideological continuity and theoretical poverty, it can appropriately be labelled, economic determinism, New-Frontier-style (Pessen, 1969; Gatell, 1970, 1967).

To try in a few paragraphs to present an adequate critique of New Frontier economic determinism would be absurd. My real purpose is to emphasize that economic determinism has revived, in large measure, because explicit, comprehensive noneconomic determinist theories have not yet been developed.

To kill economic determinism dead so that it stays dead in American historiography, its opponents must consciously, positively work to develop a body of fruitful theory that can effectively guide empirical research focused on group cohesion and social and ideological conflict. And, in my judgment, that can best be done by eliminating the economic determinist strain in Marx and de Tocqueville, combining and extending their fruitful ideas, and incorporating them into the developing body of reference group theory.

To speed the process of translating generalized exhortation into concrete, practical work, I imitate Marx and sketch below what facetiously might be called "Theses on Marx and de Tocqueville."

PROPOSITIONS ABOUT RELATIVELY LOW SOCIAL CLASS COHESION AND LOW SOCIAL CLASS CONFLICT

We might eventually develop credible propositions if we systematically combined and extended Marx and de Tocqueville, and, in the process, liberated their theories from economic determinism. My aim is to illustrate this point rather than prove it, which can best be achieved by concentrating on propositions about the low occurrence of either social class cohesion or social class conflict.

All the propositions below should be read as asserting, "other things being equal." As everyone knows, "other things" rarely, if ever, actually are equal. The propositions assert, therefore, the effect of the specified independent variable(s) on the dependent variable(s), as if they alone determined behavior. The propositions emphatically should *not* be read as predictions that low social class cohesion and conflict *invariably* will occur when the specified conditions occur. In particular situations, other independent variables may be present that counterbalance or overbalance them. Like all propositions of this type, they suggest tendencies, they do not make predictions.

   (1) The greater (and longer) the equality in legal status conditions, the less the social class cohesion and social class conflict.

This proposition derives directly from de Tocqueville. His main contribution to modern social theory was to recognize and emphasize the key role played by legal distinctions (what Marx called political distinctions) in the formation and cohesion of social groups. Conversely, I think that Marx seriously erred when he assumed that, no matter what legal relations of social existence occurred, the relations of production would inevitably produce social classes. (As is generally true of Marx's errors, this one partly resulted from his overreaction to Hegel and his overreliance upon Feuerbach's "inversion" method of analysis and criticism.)

(2) The more capitalist the economy, the more diversified the economy, the greater the geographic specialization of economic activity, the greater the range of income and the number of income strata, the less the social class cohesion and social class conflict.

Given the strong relationships he postulated between economic existence and consciousness, Marx should have asserted proposition 2. He did not—partly because he created the concept of "relative deprivation" to justify his two-class model of capitalist society (capitalist-worker).

Even if the absolute standard of living of workers continued to rise, Marx theorized, the wealth and income gap between them and capitalists would continue to widen. In relative terms, therefore, workers would continually be worse off than before. As a result, class consciousness inevitably would grow as capitalism grew (Marx and Engels, 1968: 72-94).

Ideology seems to have kept Marx from seeing the full implications of the brilliant social-psychological insights that led him to construct the concept, relative deprivation. He failed to see that as capitalism grew, relative aggrandizement would also tend to grow. (I have created that term to suggest the complementarity of the concepts and their common origin in Marx.) Had he seen this tendency, he might have predicted that relative aggrandizement in capitalist societies would develop somewhat along the following lines:

In a specified society, suppose a considerable number of economic strata developed. Suppose the standard of living of significant percentages of noncapitalists rose much faster than that of other noncapitalists, although much more slowly than that of capitalists. At any specified time then, compared to noncapitalists below them on the economic scale, *as well as to themselves, or to their parents, at some previous time,* relatively fast risers would feel relatively aggrandized. (Americans generally, American immigrants particularly, "instinctively" make such comparisons—a "social fact" seriously neglected by American economic determinists who deny the existence of significant social mobility.) Compared to fast-rising capitalists, fast-rising noncapitalists might, of course, feel relatively deprived. Under such conditions, however, it seems highly probable that significant proportions of noncapitalists would take individual capitalists, and capitalists as a group, as positive reference individuals and as a positive reference group—and the "fellow workers" below them as a negative reference group.

Space prevents my elaborating the concept of relative aggrandizement, suggesting its theoretical possibilities, or illustrating its great usefulness for American historians. Here I simply note my belief that it can powerfully contribute to the development of reference group theory and that, like the concept of relative deprivation, it logically derives from Marx's brilliant social psychological insights.

(3) The greater the perceived gross social mobility, the less the social class cohesion and social class conflict.

Gross social mobility refers to all up-and-down movement from one stratum of a stratification system to another, as well as to similar movement in all the different types of stratification systems of a society defined by some significant variable—e.g., wealth, income, occupation, power, multidimensional "status." Gross social mobility radically differs from net social mobility. The latter concept refers to changes in the percentage distribution of strata from one time to another, not to the movement of individuals from one stratum to another. A tremendous amount of counter-balancing gross social mobility might occur from one time to another, therefore, and yet produce no net social mobility (Barber and Barber, 1965). (Unfortunately, American historians of social mobility tend to ignore the basic differences between the phenomena referred to by the two different concepts—a conceptual flaw particularly characteristic of New Frontier economic determinists and fatal to their work.)

Closely analyzed, Marx's theory of social classes in capitalist societies assumed relatively little upward mobility. Social class consciousness, he recognized, depended upon hereditary membership in economic classes. Thus, I derive the following proposition from Marx: no *hereditary economic classes in advanced capitalist societies, no social classes in advanced capitalist societies.* (Economic interest groups might exist, but not social classes. In the abstract typology I have developed, social classes, when and if they existed, would be treated as one concrete form of communal group.)

In a sense, Marx's erroneous predictions about the development of social classes in capitalist societies stem less from his theoretical errors than from his empirical errors. He simply assumed, erroneously, that all capitalist societies (eventually including the United States) would produce hereditary economic classes. (As Engels observed in the 1890s, he and Marx had made serious errors in their economic history.)

The job of measuring gross and net social mobility over long time periods in capitalist societies is staggering. It poses mind-boggling conceptual and methodological problems, to say nothing of empirical problems (e.g., securing data about the social mobility of "movers," as well as "stayers"). As a result, I know of no historical study whose findings, when critically examined, can be said to be highly (or even moderately) credible. I think it more practical, therefore, as well as more theoretically significant, to concentrate on perceived gross social mobility (in relative terms, a less difficult phenomenon to study).

The third proposition asserted above rests on an assumption that seems reasonable: if gross social mobility is perceived to be high in a society, both those who really "make it" and those who do not will strongly tend to praise or blame *themselves*. Thus, the proposition is logically consistent with Marx's recognition of the importance of hereditary membership in economic classes. It can be restated in Tocquevillian form: *the greater the perceived gross social mobility, the greater the atomistic egoism.*

(4) The greater the physical mobility, the less the social class cohesion and social class conflict.

Marx recognized clearly that, in capitalist societies, conflict, not cooperation, was what might be called the natural relationship between individuals who shared similar economic attributes. But he assumed that continuous interclass conflict would overcome the natural tendency toward intraclass conflict. Inevitably, therefore, he theorized, interclass conflict would produce social classes.

But in advanced capitalist societies, as Marx correctly predicted, physical mobility tends to be high. Thus, with respect to social class cohesion and social class conflict, it tends to have something like the complex effects of high social mobility. Physical mobility particularly tends toward low class cohesion and conflict when it produces multicultural societies and communities. And from his mode of production theory, Marx could have correctly predicted that capitalist societies would increasingly tend to become multicultural societies (Benson, 1972: 307-326). Proposition 5 considers some consequences of that phenomenon.

(5) The greater and more continuous the immigration from societies whose cultural patterns are antagonistic to each others' and to those of groups in the "host country," the greater and more continuous the intrasocietal migration from areas with antagonistic cultural patterns, the less the social class cohesion and social class conflict.

It only seems necessary to emphasize here that continuing immigrant ties with "old countries" and continuing migrant ties to "old regions," continuing visible conflicts among old countries and continuing visible conflicts among old regions, all strengthen the "forces" producing low social class cohesion and low social class conflict. This proposition assumes that, when conflicting cultural patterns cut across economic class lines, the development or maintenance of social classes becomes particularly difficult. The rationale for that proposition is further developed in proposition 6.

(6) The more heterogeneous the ethnocultural and religious composition, the more developed the communication system, the less the social class cohesion and social class conflict.

Leaders of ethnocultural and religious groups correctly tend to believe that the cohesiveness, even the existence of their groups, is gravely threatened by continuous exposure of their members to different, and therefore competing, value systems and life styles. Mere knowledge that different value systems and life styles exist undermines unquestioned acceptance of a particular group's value system(s) and life style(s). When the members of an ethnocultural or religious group question the superiority of the value system(s) and life style(s) that define and bound it, at least some of its leaders become alarmed. They then act to reinforce group cohesion by developing and implementing strategies designed to overcome intragroup divisions related to differences in economic attributes.

(7) The greater the present legal equality of status condition, the less the previous inequalities of legal status, the less the informal or extralegal survivals of previous inequalities, the less the social cohesion and social class conflict.

That proposition, in effect, was frequently invoked by Marx and Engels to account for what they regarded as the deplorable immaturity of the working class in the United States. Thus, in 1886, Engels (Marx and Engels, 1942: 448-449; italics in original) described America as a society "with purely *bourgeois* institutions unleavened by feudal remnants or monarchical traditions and without a permanent and hereditary proletariate." And, in 1890 (Marx and Engels, 1942: 466-467; italics in original), though optimistic that advancing industrialization would produce the conditions needed to develop working-class consciousness, he perceptively characterized Americans as "born conservatives—just *because* America is so purely bourgeois, so entirely without a feudal past and therefore proud of its purely bourgeois organization—and so they will only get quit of the old traditional mental rubbish by practical experience" (see also Marx and Engels, 1963: 257-258. American historians who scorn what they caricature as "consensus historiography" and who ringlingly proclaim the existence of "native American radicalism" and profoundly ideological "class conflicts," unfortunately, have not read Marx and Engels carefully).

(8) The more fully capitalist the relations of production, the more fully equal the legal status (at least of males), the greater the tendency for the dominant value to be the legitimacy of individual competition for highest rank in the stratification system defined by wealth, the less the social class cohesion and social class conflict, the greater the normlessness, and the greater the pervasiveness of "identity crises."

Proposition 8 invokes a number of complex concepts whose meaning is anything but well defined, to say nothing of the measurement problems they pose. But even with no effort on my part to define those concepts, for most readers, the proposition probably has some common meaning. For the sake of argument, suppose its meaning were clear and its validity granted. We could then better understand why ethnocultural and religious attributes have strongly tended to function as the primary bases of quasi-communal and communal groups in American society. Caught up in the "rat race" of a fiercely competitive, individualistic economic system, men naturally cling or turn to ethnocultural and religious groups—to find or maintain their identity, as well as value systems to help orient their lives and life-styles to practice.

(9) And so on.

It would be possible to identify other variables that also yield potentially credible propositions about the low occurrence of social class cohesion and social class conflict. And if we verified and then combined all such propositions, of course, we then would greatly multiply their explanatory power, compared to their explanatory power when they are invoked individually. It seems clear to me, therefore, that good grounds exist to believe that Marx was fundamentally wrong when he assumed that his social class theory of conflict and cohesion applied equally well to precapitalist and capitalist societies.

In fully capitalist societies "unleavened" by precapitalist "remnants" (to use Engels' terms), social classes are "unnatural." In such societies, as Marx really knew but did not really make clear, social classes strongly tend to be works of art. Their presence, not their absence, requires imaginative, intensive, systematic research and rigorously scientific explanation.

To grant the validity of my argument does not devalue or discard Marx. On the contrary. In my judgment, his mode of production theory can incorporate the valid elements of his social class theory, as well as the valid elements of de Tocqueville's status theory. And following still another brilliant lead provided by Robert Merton, when *reconceptualized*, I believe that Marx's theories can powerfully help us to understand and explain why the alienation engendered by capitalist relations of production, particularly in highly multicultural societies, contributes to the existence of quasi-communal and communal groups based on ethnocultral and religious attributes. Marx's theories can perform that function especially well when they are further reconceptualized—namely, when they function as the materialist basis of a comprehensive theory of reference group determination of collective and individual behavior.

CONCLUSION—AND BEGINNING

To help bring about a future world of social scientific historiography that might endow human life with new discoveries and powers, I have criticized the existing historiographic world.

I have practiced ruthless criticism because I accept Marx's strategy that when "reformers" set out to find a new world, they should not attempt dogmatically to prefigure the future, but find it through criticism of the old. As he and Francis Bacon both knew, however, if we hope to get anywhere, we should have some idea of where we want to go; before we take to the road, some idea of how we expect to get there. In this essay, I have suggested where some historians should want to go. I have also suggested one way they might consider trying to get there.

NOTES

1. As I conceive the construct "social thought," it encompasses five related, but different, types of theory: (1) theory of human nature; (2) normative theory; (3) empirical theory; (4) policy theory (i.e., theories of strategies and tactics to achieve normative goals, based on specified empirical theories); (5) theory of knowledge. Theory and contribution to social thought, of course, are constructs so complex as to preclude any useful attempt to define them briefly.

2. Informed, compassionate critics will recognize that severe space limitations force me to resort blushingly to oversimplification and a mere assertion. When I expand this essay to book-length form, I will then try to develop and support my claims, not merely to assert them in oversimplified, skeletal form.

3. My reconstruction of Marx's theory of human nature owes much to a very large number of scholars, especially to brilliant works by Schaff (1970) and Israel (1971). But I have been helped most by Fromm (1971, 1969). I do, however, dissent from his argument (Fromm, 1969: 456-457; italics in original) that Marx did not theorize that the *"dynamism of human nature is primarily rooted in this need of man . . . to use the world as a means for the satisfaction of his physiological necessities."*

4. Given space limitations, I cannot try to document or justify my reconstruction of Marx's theories, or even list the very large number of scholarly works that have improved my understanding of Marx and Engels. It seems worth noting, however, that, in view of Marx's ambiguous formulations (concept formation was a post-Marxian development in the logic of social inquiry), I think it Utopian to expect that anyone can ever demonstrate that one interpretation is the only true interpretation of his theories.

5. As in the case of Marx's theories, space limitations preclude documentation or justification of my reconstruction of de Tocqueville's theories. Nor can I even list the large number of works that have proved instructive. (Comparisons are odious, but I probably have benefited most from Nisbet, 1966.)

6. In 1950, I demonstrated that Turner had uncritically taken over Achille Loria's rigidly economic determinist "free land" theory of societal evolution and given it an illogical, patriotic Midwestern twist. Subsequently, I came to realize that Loria was much less original than I thought and had grossly misappropriated and distorted Marx's ideas. (For Engels' scorching denunciation of Loria, see Marx, 1967: vol. 3, 16-19.) Turner had not read Marx and got him secondhand via Loria. Thus the famous "frontier thesis" is a distortion of a distortion—a "fact" that helps me better understand how Turner could have made such extraordinary logical and empirical errors.

As Beard was the first to acknowledge, although he later severely criticized Turner and the "frontier school" of historians, he began his economic determinist studies of American history full of praise for Turner (1965: 5). ("Under the direction of this original scholar and thinker [Turner], the influence of the material circumstances of the frontier on American politics was first clearly pointed out.") In 1960, in a lengthy critique of Beard and his critics, I suggested that he had been influenced by Loria and Marx directly, as well as indirectly via Turner. I am now even more convinced than before that Beard deliberately concealed—for laudable motives—Marx's strong influence upon him by way of E.R.A. Seligman and James Harvey Robinson. Proof of my conviction must await another occasion. For my published studies of the European origins of ideas Americanized by Turner and Beard, see Benson (1960, and 1972: 175-189.)

REFERENCES

BARBER, B. and E. BARBER [eds.] (1965) European Social Class: Stability and Change. New York: Macmillan.

BEARD, C. A. [ed.] (1965) An Economic Interpretation of the Constitution of the United States. New York: Free Press.

——— (1939) "Turner's 'the frontier in American history,'" pp. 61-74 in M. Cowley and B. Smith (eds.) Books That Changed Our Minds. New York: Doubleday, Doran.

——— (1921) "Review of Turner's frontier in American history." New Republic 25 (February 16): 349-350.

BENSON, L. (1972) Toward the Scientific Study of History. Philadelphia: J. B. Lippincott.

——— (1961) The Concept of Jacksonian Democracy: New York as a Test Case. Princeton, N.J.: Princeton Univ. Press.

——— (1960) Turner & Beard: American Historical Writing Reconsidered. New York: Free Press.

BOGUE, A. G. (1968) "United States: the 'new' political history." J. of Contemporary History 3 (January): 5-27.

BOTTOMORE, T. B. [ed.] (1964) Karl Marx: Early Writings. New York: McGraw-Hill.

——— and M. RUBEL [eds.] (1964) Karl Marx: Selected Writings in Sociology and Social Philosophy. New York: McGraw-Hill.

FEUER, L. S. [ed.] (1959) Marx and Engels: Basic Writings on Politics and Philosophy. Garden City, N.Y.: Doubleday Anchor.

Benson / GROUP COHESION AND IDEOLOGICAL CONFLICT [149]

FORFORMISANO, R. (1971) The Birth of Mass Political Parties. Princeton, N.J.: Princeton Univ. Press.

FROMM, E. (1971) Marx's Concept of Man. New York: Frederick Ungar.

——— (1969) "Marx's contribution to the knowledge of man," pp. 454-464 in International Social Science Council, Marx and Contemporary Scientific Thought. The Hague: Mouton.

GATELL, F. O. (1970) "Beyond Jacksonian consensus," pp. 350-361 in H. Bass (ed.) The State of American History. Chicago: Quadrangle.

——— (1967) "Money and party in Jacksonian America: a quantitative look at New York City's men of quality." Pol. Sci. Q. 82 (June): 235-252.

HOGBEN, L. (1961) "Darwinism and human society in retrospect," in M. Banton (ed.) Darwinism and the Study of Society. London: Tavistock.

HYMAN H. H. and E. SINGER [eds.] (1968) Readings in Reference Group Theory and Research. New York: Free Press.

ISRAEL, J. (1971) Alienation: From Marx to Modern Sociology. Boston: Allyn & Bacon.

MARX, K. (1967) Capital. New York: International.

——— (1963a) The 18th Brumaire of Louis Bonaparte. New York: International.

——— (1963b) The Poverty of Philosophy. New York: International.

——— and F. ENGELS (1968) Karl Marx and Frederick Engels: Selected Works in One Volume. New York: International.

——— (1963) Letters to Americans: 1848-1895. New York: International.

——— (1942) Selected Correspondence: 1846-1895. New York: International.

MERTON, R. K. (1968) Social Theory and Social Structure. New York: Free Press.

NISBET, R. A. (1966) The Sociological Tradition. New York: Basic Books.

PESSEN, E. (1969) Jacksonian America: Society, Personality, and Politics. Homewood, Ill.: Dorsey.

SCHAFF, A. (1970) Marxism and the Human Individual. New York: McGraw-Hill.

SCHLESINGER, A. M., Jr. (1945) The Age of Jackson. Boston: Little, Brown.

STRUIK, D. J. [ed.] (1971) Birth of the Communist Manifesto. New York: International.

SWIERENGA, R. P. (1971) "Ethnocultural political analysis: a new approach to American ethnic studies." J. of Amer. Studies 5: 59-79.

DE TOCQUEVILLE, A. (1966) Democracy in America. New York: Harper & Row.

——— (1945) Democracy in America. New York: Alfred A. Knopf.

THE AUTHORS

LEE BENSON is Professor of History of the American Peoples, University of Pennsylvania. He has served as chairman of committees of the American Historical Association and the American Council of Learned Societies and is currently a member of the Executive Committee of the American Academy of Political and Social Science. He is the author of four books, of which *Toward the Scientific Study of History* is the most recent.

ALLAN G. BOGUE is F. J. Turner Professor of History at the University of Wisconsin and Chairman of the American Historical Association's ad hoc Committee on Quantitative Data in History. He is author or an editor of five books in American economic or political history, as well as the author of various articles. His most recent publication (with W. O. Aydelotte and R. W Fogel) is *The Dimensions of Quantitative History.*

ROBERT R. DYKSTRA, Professor of History at the University of Iowa, is a former editor of *Civil War History.* His book *The Cattle Towns* was winner of a Western Heritage Award as "the Outstanding Western Non-Fiction Book of 1968." He is working at this time on two computer-aided studies of Midwestern political behavior.

J. ROGERS HOLLINGSWORTH is a Professor of History at the University of Wisconsin. He is the author of *The Whirligig of Politics: The Democracy of Cleveland and Bryan,* and editor of books on American expansion and nation-building. He has held grants from the National Endowment for the Humanities and the Rockefeller Foundation. At present his research is focused upon cross-national patterns of economic development and social and political response.

PETER D. McCLELLAND received his undergraduate degree in economics from Queens University, Kingston, Ontario, worked for two years at the Central Bank of Canada and studied philosophy at Oxford University. He received his Ph.D. in economics from Harvard University in 1966 and taught there until 1972. He is currently an Associate Professor at Cornell University.

JAMES E. WRIGHT is an Assistant Professor of History at Dartmouth College. He holds a Ph.D. (1969) from the University of Wisconsin. Yale University Press is publishing his *Politics of Populism,* and he is currently working on a study of New Hampshire Progressivism. Both these studies are concerned with models of popular voting behavior.

ROBERT ZEMSKY is Associate Professor of American Civilization at the University of Pennsylvania and the author of *Merchants, Farmers, and River Gods: An Essay on Eighteenth-Century Politics.* With Richard Jensen, he planned and offered the first summer course in quantitative methods for historians at the Inter-University Consortium for Political Research. He is especially interested in the problems involved in the development of methods and theories particularly adapted to the unique nature of historical data.